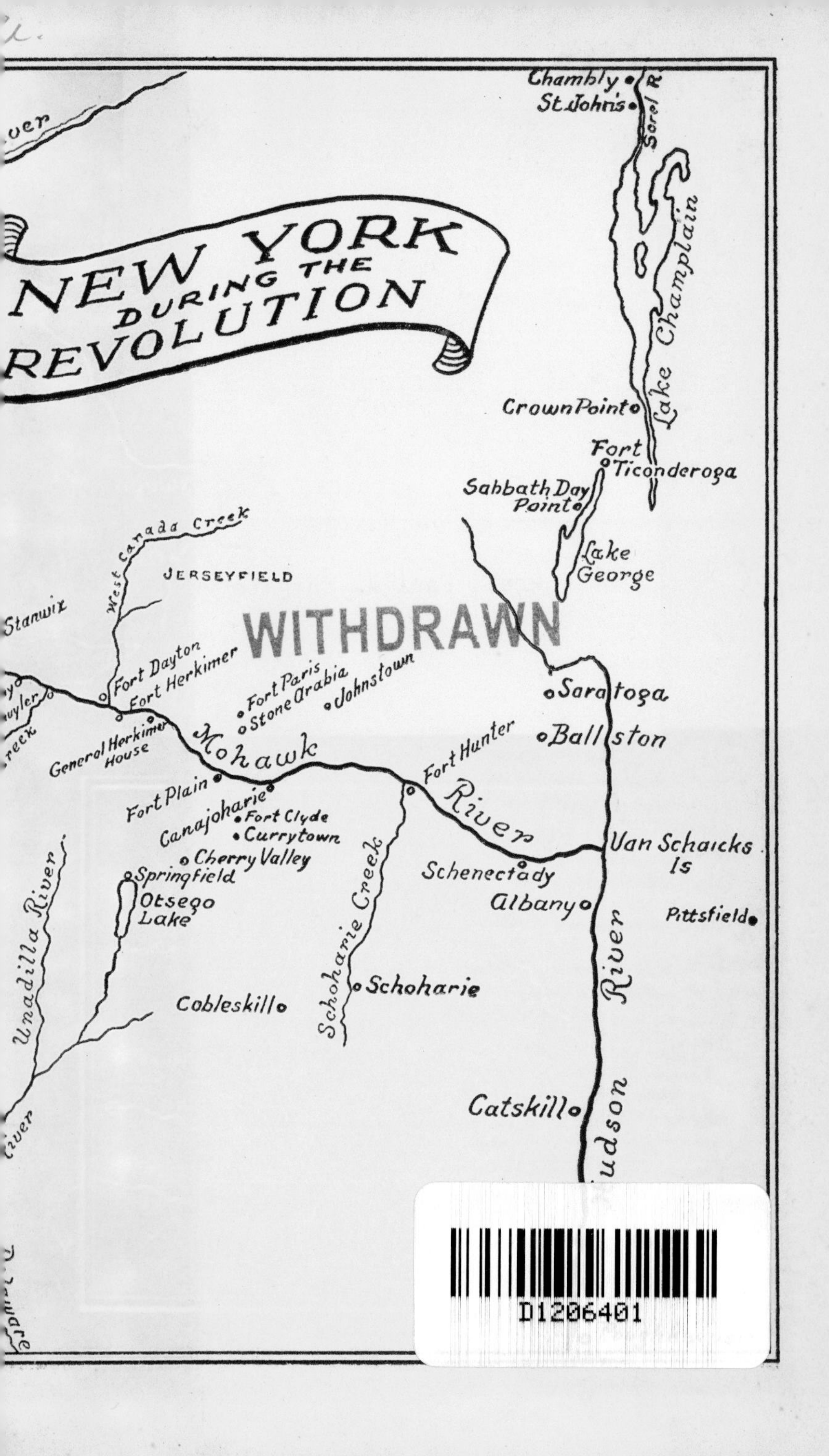
NEW YORK
DURING THE
REVOLUTION
Chambly
St. John's
Sorel R.
Lake Champlain
Crown Point
Fort
Ticonderoga
Sabbath Day
Point
Lake
George
West Canada Creek
JERSEYFIELD
Stanwix
Fort Dayton
Fort Herkimer
Fort Paris
Stone Arabia
Johnstown
General Herkimer
House
Mohawk
River
Fort Plain
Canajoharie
Fort Clyde
Currytown
Cherry Valley
Springfield
Otsego
Lake
Fort Hunter
Saratoga
Ballston
Van Schaicks
Is
Schenectady
Albany
Pittsfield
Schoharie Creek
Schoharie
Cobleskill
Unadilla River
Catskill
Hudson
River

Herkimer Camera Shop.
Herkimer, N.Y.
31 Dec. 1965

MARINUS WILLETT

Howard Thomas

REPRODUCED FROM THE ORIGINAL IN THE
NEW YORK STATE LIBRARY, ALBANY

HOWARD THOMAS

MARINUS WILLETT

SOLDIER • PATRIOT

1740 • 1830

PROSPECT BOOKS
PROSPECT, NEW YORK · 1954

LIMITED FIRST EDITION

Copy No. 1455

LIBRARY OF CONGRESS CATALOG NUMBER: 54-8876

PRINTED BY AMERICAN BOOK-STRATFORD PRESS, INC., NEW YORK

Contents

Foreword

THE AMERICAN REVOLUTION did not end with the surrender of Cornwallis at Yorktown on October 19th, 1781. A battle was fought six days later at Johnstown, New York, and was followed on October 30th by a final sharp wilderness skirmish in the snow at a place called Jerseyfield, on the West Canada Creek, eighteen miles or so above the Mohawk River. The American Commander in both these actions was Marinus Willett.

Of all the men who held regular command on the Mohawk frontier he was the only one throughout the war able to contain the British-Tory-Indian raiding forces that for five years swept down from Niagara, Oswego, and Champlain to harass the Mohawk and Schoharie settlements. When he accepted the Mohawk command—and in so doing sacrificed all personal hopes of promotion in the Continental Line—the district had lost more than two-thirds of its effective militia men. The remainder of the people, demoralized and nearly destitute, had in Governor Clinton's descriptive phrase "hutted themselves" in small forts or palisaded houses. Washington's hopes and all his energies were turning towards the south, and there were no regular troops to spare for reinforcing the northwest frontier. If it was to be held as a granary for the Continental Army and a barrier against attacks on Schenectady and Albany, the fighting effectiveness of the militia would have to be restored and courage and hope renewed among the people. Marinus Willett was the one man considered capable of doing the job.

He was a man of simple courage and singleness of purpose; he had faith in the American cause and unlike many of his brother officers was willing to put it above his own ambitions. He knew the New York frontier better probably than any other officer in the militia or the Continental Line. As a second lieutenant at the age of 18 he had served with distinction in the French and Indian war, first in Abercrombie's disastrous expedition against Ticonderoga and then on Bradstreet's brilliant dash across Lake Ontario to capture and destroy Fort Frontenac. He had been a leader of the Sons of Liberty in New York City and an outspoken voice against the oppressions of the British Government. A man of almost no formal education, he could at times express himself with natural eloquence. And he knew how to lead men.

He had been second in command at Fort Stanwix when St. Leger laid siege to it and had led the successful foray against the Tory and Indian encampments while the Battle of Oriskany was being fought. Later he had seen service with Washington in New Jersey and had played a prominent part in General Sullivan's expedition against the western Iroquois towns in 1779. Few men on either side had seen more continuous and active service, and few officers commanded more firmly the respect and loyalty of the troops under them.

When the peace was signed in 1783, Marinus Willett was forty-three years old. Forty-seven years of life remained to him and during this second span he was active in politics, held various public offices, and undertook successfully a difficult mission to the Creek Indians. He amassed a respectable fortune; and although he was unsuccessful and inept in his political ventures, when he died ten thousand citizens of New York came to his funeral.

At the end the simple virtues of his patriotism, his courage as a soldier, and his undeviating loyalty to his country were remembered. He has long deserved more attention from historians, and Mr. Thomas has done us a service by giving us this straightforward account of his career.

WALTER D. EDMONDS

I

REVEILLE

1740 — 1775

Young Rebel

PANDEMONIUM RULED THE FLY MARKET. Men raced through Wall Street and Maiden Lane: some did not stop until they reached Broadway; others dodged down side streets and into doorways. A few stood their ground, their canes grasped in firm hands. Windows along Wall Street flew open, permitting excited women to exchange rumors across the narrow lane. High and piercing rang the cry, "The press gang! The press gang!" It echoed from the gabled houses that led to Broadway.

A boy watering horses at the Province Arms, a rambling tavern near Trinity Church, heard the cries and understood their meaning. France was challenging English supremacy of the seas. The British needed sailors to man their ships. Able seamen could be found in the lodging houses near the Fly Market. Some might be deserters from British ships, but impressment gangs took men indiscriminately. Sailors had landed at Murray's Wharf. They would be hurrying through the Fly Market, seizing citizens despite their protests, forcing them to the boats.

The boy dropped his pail. His long legs raced down Wall Street, careless that one stocking had relinquished its alliance with his knee-breeches and had tangled with the buckle of one shoe. The wind ballooned his white shirt, while his pigtail rode horizontally, its black ribbon flapping against his neck and shoulders. The boy held his fists clenched at his chest, sending a rush of color to his cheeks. His tightly-set lips stretched white above a chin which rode ahead like the prow of a man-of-war. His breath came through his hawk nose in sharp inhalations and a glint of anger added steel to his gray eyes.

People ran in all directions. Fear, consternation and anger were registered on their faces. The boy wove his way between them, now brushing aside a retreating citizen, now altering his course to seek an opening through which he could dash. He was not running away from danger; he was hurrying toward it with all the speed he could muster.

The Fly Market opened up before him, wide, spacious, its stalls snuggled around the square. Tables had been overturned and abandoned. The cobblestones were littered with fish and vegetables. A man ran toward Wall Street, his coat torn, his face red with exertion. At his heels sprinted three sailors, one of whom threw himself at the fleeing man. His arms encircled the fugitive's legs, bringing him to the pavement with a sickening thud. The three sailors pounced upon their prostrate victim and pummelled his head and shoulders with sticks until he lay still. One of them bound the unconscious captive with stout ropes while his companions stood guard.

The boy from the Province Arms stood at the entrance to the Fly Market, his fists balled at his sides, his breath coming in gasps between clenched teeth. Perspiration poured from his forehead and rolled down his cheeks. A different kind of sweat dampened his armpits, a wetness caused not so much by exertion as by the horror spread before him.

The victim had fallen almost at the boy's feet. Blood streamed from a cut on his face, which looked whiter than the cobblestones. His body hung limp when two sailors raised it in their arms. Other seamen appeared, brandishing clubs and pistols. The whole party moved toward the wharf, shouting taunts at the citizens who had gathered against the walls of the buildings.

The boy stood there, fascinated. His eyes swept the market, catching the groups of men who stood by, consumed with anger, yet unwilling to lend aid to their fellow citizen. Canes were grasped in hands whose knuckles showed white. Jaws were set in disapproval. But no move was made to intercept the British seamen, who rowed away in boats which contained several trussed victims.

A buzzing of voices sounded in the Fly Market. Groups of citizens gathered to gesticulate fiercely and to raise their voices in protest. Women shrieked from opened windows. And several small boys, braver than their elders, rushed to hurl stones at the departing boats.

The boy from the Province Arms did not join them. At fifteen he considered himself a man. He had witnessed a brutal attack on New York citizens by an impressment gang. All around him had stood able-bodied men armed with canes, some of them with more effective weapons bulging from their pockets, yet not one had dared to challenge this piece of British effrontery. And the boy himself, tall, angular and strong, had been equally helpless to repel this violation of the freedom of American colonists.

Yet he, Marinus Willett, had learned one lesson; that British tyranny must be stopped, even though opposition might lead to war and ruin.

The Willetts were among the early settlers of Flushing, Long Island. Colonel Thomas Willett, the boy's great-grandfather, gained reputations in several branches of activity. He served as captain of the Queens County militia in 1673, when the approach of a Dutch fleet alarmed New York. Willett at Jamaica received an order to draw up his troops to New Utrecht "to make discovery or to give assistance." The Governor was away visiting the Governor of Massachusetts. The city lay defenseless. Some Dutchmen rowed out to Sandy Hook and gave the admiral assurances that New York could be taken. The fleet sailed into the harbor and the city surrendered on July 30. In 1687 Colonel Willett and a group of militia were sent up the Hudson to defend Schenectady.

Upon his return he was appointed High Sheriff of Queens County, an office which he held for eleven years. In this capacity he settled, among other things, the boundary between Flushing and Jamaica. For the next nine years he served as a member of the Governor's Council in New York. In 1701 he and John Tallman were elected to the Assembly but they did not last long. They sent in a petition which said in part: "Till you giv us furder satisfaktion and the speaker clere himself from being an aliane, we cannot acte with you, to sit and spend ower time and the countries mony to macke actes that will be voyd in themselves and we consider you no house." This barbarous language angered the Assembly. Willett and Tallman were expelled for their insolence. Willett, however, was a member at the time of his death in 1725.

His son, Elbert, who resided in Jamaica, also served the public as sheriff at the time of his death in 1705, while his grandson, Edward, the father of Marinus, was brought up in the home of an uncle who held the office of High Sheriff.

Edward Willett boasted some education, and Alletta Clowes, whom he married, was the daughter of a prominent Jamaica lawyer. Of the thirteen children born to the couple, only three lived to see the American Revolution. Marinus, the eleventh child and the youngest of six boys, was born at Jamaica, July 31, 1740.

Though Edward Willett supported his family by farming, he also taught in the parochial school at Grace Church, Jamaica. He was evidently a satisfactory teacher, for five years after the school had been opened he had 43 pupils, was paid a salary of £15 a year and commended for his exemplary life and diligence. His name may be found among the original pew-holders of the new Grace Church.

Little is known of Marinus Willett's early life. It is probable that he went to the parochial school in Jamaica. That he attended church regularly as a lad is pretty certain. Of his other activities there is no written record.

Jamaica, the county seat, possessed a courthouse and three churches. It was also a marketing center. When Marinus was four years old a slight earthquake shook the island and the proclamation of war against France was published at the courthouse. Two years later, during the midst of a smallpox epidemic, the Queens County militia marched out of Jamaica to embark for Albany and Canada.

In 1749 Edward Willett moved to New York City, where he took over the proprietorship of the Horse and Manger, a tavern at the foot of James Street on the East River near the slaughterhouse. Three years later he "revived" the Horse and Cart, an inn on William Street much patronized by traders from New England. On October 25, 1753 the Supreme Court, after closing its session, marched from the City Hall to the home of Lieutenant Governor James De Lancey and escorted him to the Horse and Cart, where a "grand dimmer" *(sic)* was served. The next year Willett shifted his business to the De Lancey mansion, the owner having moved to his new country seat at Corlear's Hook. The two-story building, in excellent condition, with gardens sloping down to the Hudson, was located near the Oswego Market and close to Trinity Church. Willett named it The Sign of the New York Arms, but to New Yorkers it was familiarly known as the Province Arms. It was destined to be the most important hostelry in the city for several decades, being replaced in 1794 by the City Hotel, which also had a long and memorable history.

Edward Willett being a staunch supporter of the British crown, his inn became the scene of several notable receptions. In April, 1755 Governors William Shirley of Massachusetts and Robert Hunter Morris of Pennsylvania were entertained by James De Lancey, who met his guests at Whitehall Slip and escorted them through decorated streets to the Province Arms, where a dinner was enjoyed and the health of His Majesty and the royal family was drunk. A year later the governors of King's College, after laying the cornerstone of New York's first institution for higher learning, returned to Willett's hostelry for a sumptuous repast and met there the next day for their first business session.

The year 1755 depressed New York. The news of General Braddock's defeat had thrown the city into gloom. The streets were full of British soldiers passing to and from the war. The drum-beat sounded familiar to the fashionable citizens who promenaded each afternoon in front of Trinity Church. On September 3 the sound of cannon from the harbor threw the people into a panic that was soon relieved by joy. The sloop *Sphinx* had arrived during the night with Sir Charles Hardy, the new Governor, who was escorted to the fort and then to the Province Arms, where De Lancey entertained him munificently and more toasts were drunk to the King. Several hampers of Madeira had been provided for the populace at The Fields, a gathering-place on the outskirts of the city. Bonfires were lighted in the evening. To climax the occasion, the Governor appeared before the people to say a few words.

The family which Edward Willett moved over from Jamaica had been depleted by death and marriage. Two children had died before Marinus' birth. Two others were buried in Grace Church graveyard before 1750. Isaac, one of the older brothers, was married and the father of children. It is also possible that Samuel and Edward were heads of families. In 1755 there were five children under age: Margaret 19, Elbert 17, Marinus 15, Catherine 8, and Joanna 5. They probably constituted the Willett family at the Province Arms.

The city was concentrated at the tip of Manhattan Island. Of the 13,000 inhabitants, 2000 were Negroes. About 2500 buildings lined the narrow, winding streets, some of which were paved with cobblestones, while others were muddy lanes. New York merchants exported to the British West Indies quantities of bread, peas, rye, Indian corn, apples, onions, boards, staves, horses, sheep, butter, cheese, pickled oysters, beef and pork. In return they received rum, sugar and molasses and some cotton from St. Thomas. Logs and flaxseed were exported to England and Ireland in exchange for dry goods, the balance of trade remaining in the hands of the mother country.

It was natural that a lad of fifteen should be fascinated by the sea. And Marinus Willett's brother Isaac was serving aboard a privateer, thus adding to the youngster's interest in shipping. Hence Marinus' repeated trips to the wharves and his witnessing the impressment which caused his everlasting hatred for British methods of coercion.

Talk of war occupied all tongues. General Braddock's disgrace was forgotten in the publicity given to the young Virginian who had offered him such excellent advice, only to have it refused by the arrogant Englishman. Colonel George Washington, twenty-four years of age, passed through New York in 1756 en route to Massachusetts to lay before Governor Shirley a memorial from the officers of Virginia respecting difficulties in rank which had arisen among them. The young officer arrived in New York in February and spent a week in the city. He also lingered briefly on his return to Virginia.

His party, which consisted of two captains of the Virginia light horse and several servants, dazzled New York. The officers wore British scarlet, with gold-laced hats adorning their powdered heads. Their swords bore decorations of gold and scarlet. The Washington coat-of-arms appeared prominently on the fittings of the horses. The servants wore special livery imported from England. White coats, faced with scarlet, and scarlet waistcoats stretched across their chests.

New Yorkers were accustomed to British finery, but these young Virginians outstripped any other sartorial creations they had seen, so the party was greeted with enthusiasm everywhere it went.

Marinus Willett saw Washington several times. On each occasion he became more impressed with the tall young man whose long legs gripped the horse he rode so easily. Dignity rested deep in the pock-marked face beneath the gay hat of scarlet and gold, and the dark blue eyes scanned the crowds steadily and thoughtfully. Occasionally a trace of a smile would break the firm line of Washington's wide mouth, but for the most part he stared straight ahead, his eyes focused on some vision which he alone could grasp. The cheers disturbed him not. He seemed to know that he was riding toward destiny.

Marinus Willett ranked Washington next to God. Later in life he was inclined to elevate his hero to first place, but at sixteen he was a devout member of Trinity Church. Edward Willett had brought up his family under Episcopalian doctrine, both in Jamaica and in New York. The family pew was filled each Sunday and Mrs. Willett took the children regularly to Dr. Barclay's house for a study of the catechism. Edward Willett, though he sold liquor at the Province Arms, never permitted his children to touch it. He told them of his own experience. As a youth he had purchased some cordial which had an agreeable taste. On two successive mornings he had taken glasses of the liquor, which had tasted delicious. On the third morning he again filled a glass, but something made him refrain from draining its contents. It was apprehension of the danger which might come to him if he became addicted to the habit of dram-drinking. He never touched liquor from that day and he instilled into his children a disgust for drunkenness which carried through Marinus' long life.

But nothing could prevent the lad from being intoxicated

by George Washington. The vision of the Virginian danced constantly before him. Marinus pictured himself fighting at the side of the tall colonel, protecting him from danger, helping him to drive the French and Indians away from the borders. Isaac was out fighting the French at sea. Why couldn't Marinus enlist in the army? He was a Willett and Willetts had fought in all the colonial wars. He was strong and tall for his age.

He had two years to wait.

Scarcely had Washington departed for the South, when the Earl of Loudoun arrived with 2400 men whom he expected to billet on the city. The corporation informed the pompous Britisher that free quarters were against the common law and a violation of the Petition of Right.

"God damn my blood!" exclaimed the irate Loudoun to the Mayor. "If you won't billet my officers upon free quarters this day, I'll order all the troops in North America under my command and billet them myself in this city."

A subscription was raised to billet the officers, while Loudoun sailed for Boston to breathe more threats. The presence of the soldiers brought bickering and friction, but the gay uniforms added color to the social functions of the city. The theaters took on new gaiety and entertainments in the taverns were brighter because of the presence of the British officers.

Officer in Green

IN JANUARY, 1758 Marinus Willett became second lieutenant in a company formed by Captain Thomas Williams of Long Island, a "man of activity and courage." The eighteen-year-old's uniform consisted of a green coat trimmed with silver twist, white underclothes and black gaiters. The cocked hat bore a large black cockade of silk ribbon, together with a silver button and a loop. There probably was no prouder young man in the world than Marinus Willett when Oliver De Lancey's battalion embarked for Albany in May.

They marched to protect Schenectady. The day was hot, the road sandy, the pace relentless. Willett trudged along, his underclothes dark with sweat, his gaiters brown from the dust. His rifle and pack seemed to weigh a thousand pounds. His throat felt dry as sandpaper. Soldiering, after all, was more than fighting battles. At the close of the day he threw himself on the ground, completely exhausted.

The danger in the Mohawk Valley was over in a fortnight, so the New Yorkers marched to the foot of Lake George. Here Willett encountered another hero. Lord Howe, who was gathering his forces for a movement to the north, would command respect anywhere. His carriage was unassuming, his deportment modest, his manner easy. Prepared for a campaign in the wilderness, he was dressed in a loose ammunition shirt. His hair had been cropped short. Orders had been issued for all others to do likewise. Long coats were a handicap in the wilderness; their skirts caught on every bramble. Special leggings of buckskin replaced the white parade trousers of the regulars; these would be better protection against the stings of insects. Howe eliminated camp tables and chairs and cut down the baggage to a minimum. A story went the rounds of the camp. While the army was in Albany, Howe invited his officers to have lunch with him in his tent. There were no chairs, only a few logs thrown on the ground. Howe sat down on one of the logs and motioned for his guests to do likewise. Pork and beans were served, without implements with which to eat them. Howe produced several sheaths containing rude knives and forks, which he presented to the officers without comment. He also gave each officer a quantity of powdered ginger with the orders that when the troops came to a stream they were not to lie down on their stomachs to drink, but were to dip the water from the stream with their cups and put a pinch of ginger into it. Too many soldiers had died in the past from drinking brackish water. A prone soldier also made an excellent target for a prowling Indian.

On June 5 nearly 16,000 troops embarked for Fort Ticonderoga, which the French called Fort Carillon. General James Abercrombie had the command, but Howe was the life and soul of the army. In the same boat with Howe rode Colonel John Bradstreet, a picturesque figure who had been at the siege of Louisburg and had held the post of Lieutenant Governor of St. John's, Newfoundland. A fleet of 900 batteaux, 135 whaleboats and a large number of flats sailed in stately procession up Lake George.

At sundown the party landed at Sabbath Day Point, where the soldiers dug holes in the sand and mounted camp kettles. A row of fires dotted the shore and printed their wavering reflections upon the darkening water. The troops were rowed up the lake at midnight and landed at the northern end as dawn was breaking over the Vermont hills.

A small French post was attacked and taken. Marinus Willett took no part in the brief skirmish, but he beheld for the first time a sight which filled him with disgust. Two Stockbridge Indians appeared in camp with the reeking scalps of two French soldiers. Willett vowed he would never permit scalping if he could avoid it.

The advance toward Ticonderoga started in good order, the regiments marching through the woods as compactly as possible, in the approved British manner. Few of De Lancey's New Yorkers had experienced battle. Years later Marinus Willett recorded the emotions he felt as he approached the first battle of his career. He did not experience fear, but was "governed by an enthusiasm with which soldiers cannot be too much inspired when entering into action, indeed more or less of this enthusiasm should govern every step of a soldier desirous of atchieving fame. The sentiment common in the army that he is a good soldier who does what he is ordered will seldom procure that fame which ought to be the soldiers glory. To arrive at this goal it is necessary not only to obey orders but to seek occasions of performing enterprises by voluntary services and by projecting plans for annoying the enemy."

A volley of shots shattered the morning air. Howe spurred his horse to the front. The whole force advanced with enthusiasm and confidence, inspired by the leader's example. A force Willett estimated at 1000 French regulars was dispersed, but a lone Indian caused more trouble than the entire enemy detachment. From behind a tree he fired the shot which killed Lord Howe.

The British, rushing forward, became entangled in the underbrush. Wandering parties fired at each other, thinking they were attacking the enemy. The whole force, leaderless, got a severe attack of the jitters. The mere shaking of a leaf would set a whole line of troops firing—or running. A large group charged into the river; some men were nearly drowned.

Companies became disorganized. No man seemed to know where he was or where he belonged. The army disintegrated into rabble wandering from place to place, alternately hiding behind trees or taking blind shots at suspected enemies.

Willett's company had fled helter-skelter at the news of Howe's death. It was hopeless to try to organize them. It would be better to catch any men as they came along and gather them to defend against a possible French counter-attack. In this task the young lieutenant enlisted the aid of an Irishman named Thomas Muncey, who had seen service in the regular army. Between them they collected several hundred men and marched them back toward the boats in some semblance of order.

They found General Abercrombie standing under a huge tree, his aging form wrapped in a large cloak. Two regiments were drawn up in battle array to protect him.

Night fell. Willett and Muncey halted the frightened troops in a wooded spot. No fires were lighted. The troops huddled together to keep warm. Morning found them near the spot where the late action had commenced. Naked soldiers lay on the ground where Indians had killed, scalped and stripped them. Some were French; others were friends and relatives. Sadly, the remnants of the army marched back to the lake.

They were on the march again at noon. They camped for the night within three miles of Fort Ticonderoga. Sir William Johnson arrived with 600 Iroquois, who crossed the river and mounted the heights. Scalp-yells rang against the woods; bullets spattered against the French fortifications. French soldiers, accustomed to such performances, refused to be cowed. At nine in the morning the army marched against the fort, intending to strike the French before they were prepared.

General Montcalm, in command of Fort Carillon, had taken advantage of Abercrombie's delay. Trees had been toppled by thousands. Their tops had been lopped off and their trunks piled to form a barricade which zig-zagged along the top of a ridge less than a mile from the fort. Notches had been cut in the upper logs for loopholes and before the barricade a swath had been cut in the forest to the distance of a musket shot. Trees had been left where they had fallen.

Willett and his men were caught in the open space before the enemy breastwork. Three British regiments were moving in from the right, struggling to extricate themselves from the underbrush. They stormed the breastwork with fixed bayonets, while the French calmly shot them down. For five hours the struggle went on under a hot summer sun. The British withdrew at dusk without any semblance of order, leaving their dead and wounded on the field.

Willett and thirty men retired to a hill a mile distant, kindled fires and refreshed themselves with water and biscuits. It had been a frightful day for these New Yorkers. Several of their comrades lay dead before the French breastwork; some thrashed through the forest aimlessly, together with half of Abercrombie's army. Campfires flashed here and there without order. Willett, tired and disgusted, fell into a fretful sleep, from which he was aroused at dawn and informed that the troops were retreating toward Lake George. Two thousand men had been killed, wounded, or captured. Fourteen thousand remained, due to the efforts of Colonel John Bradstreet, who had stood on the shore to prevent the men from rushing pell-mell into the boats. He was opposed to retreating after an initial setback, but Abercrombie had given the order, so the flotilla which had sailed four days before with such confidence now rowed disconsolately down the lake. The campaign had been an absolute failure. The British leaders, with the exception of Howe and Bradstreet, had no conception of warfare that was not fought in an open field and they would not heed advice from men who knew something about frontier fighting. Braddock had led his redcoats into an ambush despite Washington's warning. Abercrombie was retreating, refusing to listen to Colonel Bradstreet. Stupidity and pride were the great drawbacks of the British. Willett learned a lesson which he did not forget.

With Bradstreet against Frontenac

COLONEL BRADSTREET PLEADED with General Abercrombie for a chance to lead an expedition against Fort Frontenac on Lake Ontario. Abercrombie called a council of war at the foot of Lake George. He announced that he would go back to Albany and prepare for next year's campaign. Bradstreet had a stubborn streak. He weakened Abercrombie and gained his consent to march against Fort Frontenac.

He and 3000 men advanced up the Mohawk Valley the following morning. He had only one company of British regulars and a company of artillery. The rest of the soldiers were provincials.

Willett's company did not go on the expedition, so it may be that the young New Yorker volunteered. Anyway, he marched with Bradstreet, together with Thomas Arrowhead, "an active and capable captain."

They forded the Schoharie Creek at Fort Hunter and passed through the fertile Mohawk Valley. The hay and grain stood ripe in the clearings. German and Dutch settlers paused before their cabins to cheer the soldiers. Red-cheeked girls waved their kerchiefs.

Fort Herkimer, the frontier outpost, was a three-story stone house with portholes at each story. It was surrounded by a ditch and palisades. Captain Nicholas Herkimer had left it late in April to repel an enemy attack. The frontier felt safe. Herkimer did not hide in a fort like a Britisher and let the Indians ravage the countryside. The people of the German Flatts, rebuilding their charred cabins along the Mohawk, looked upon the sturdy German as the saviour of the Valley.

At the Oneida Carrying Place, the mile and a half of portage between the Mohawk River and Wood Creek, General John Stanwix was erecting a new fort. The British had built three forts at this strategic point. Two years earlier the French had skated up the St. Lawrence to Fort Presentation, changed to snowshoes and struck south over Indian trails toward the Carrying Place. With cries of "Vive le Roi!" they had rushed into Fort Bull, killed sixty men and taken thirty prisoners. The fort had been levelled to the ground. Colonel Daniel Webb, marching to the relief of Oswego that summer, had lost his courage. He had halted at the Carrying Place, burned the two other forts, felled some logs across Wood Creek and retreated down the Valley. The British were spending $266,000 on the new fort, which was to be named Stanwix after its builder.

Bradstreet stayed two weeks at the Carrying Place, building a dam on Wood Creek to raise the waters, which ran at summer depth. The batteaux and provisions also had to be dragged from the Mohawk to the creek. The dam was opened, but the low water and Webb's logs made passage slow for the batteaux, so six days were consumed reaching Oswego, where Bradstreet halted to inspect his troops and repair damages to the boats incurred during the portage around Oswego Falls.

Fort Frontenac was the connecting link between the French capital at Quebec and the frontier outpost at Niagara. Its destruction would be a severe blow to the French cause. Bradstreet planned his attack carefully. The flotilla rowed up Lake Ontario for three days and landed in the night about two miles from Fort Frontenac. Men were sent into the woods the following morning to make fascines and gabions. Two small mortars were landed and erected about three quarters of a mile from the fort. An exchange of shots resulted. Toward evening a loud explosion rose from the fort and smoke began to curl above the piled logs.

Bradstreet took the initiative. Nine hundred men advanced through a hollow, out of range of the fort's cannon. Each man carried a bundle of fascines in his hand; every two men carried between them a gabion on a pole. They commenced to erect a breastwork on an eminence about 175 yards from the fort. Marinus Willett was in the party chosen for this hazardous task. Unavoidable noise attracted the enemy's fire. Grape-shot and musketry sounded in the night. Several men were killed or wounded. But the work went on. By morning Bradstreet's battery commanded Fort Frontenac. A brig lying in the port tried to sail away but was forced ashore by accurate shots from the battery. At nine the beating of the chamade sounded from the fort and a white flag appeared on the ramparts. The explosion of the day before had occurred in the magazine and had blown a part of the walls away. The fort, hopelessly outnumbered and badly damaged, surrendered with all of its stores.

The afternoon was spent in destroying the works. Two vessels were loaded with loot; seven others in the port were blown up. At Oswego the captured boats were unloaded and set afire. The expedition had accomplished its purpose with the loss of one man killed and eleven wounded. Marinus Willett learned from Colonel Bradstreet that defensive warfare would not win victories. The British officer went out after the enemy rather than permitting them to come to him.

If the tall New York youth had been patting himself on the back because he had been through two campaigns without injury, he was soon to regret his optimism. At Oswego Falls the soldiers, fatigued after their arduous trip from Frontenac, ate too ravenously of half-cooked meat. Dysentery overtook the victorious army. Men sickened and died. During the three days at Oswego Falls one hundred men were buried. By the time the army reached the ruins of Fort Bull one half of the soldiers were unfit for service. It took four days, with the help of General Stanwix and his soldiers, for the enfeebled men to get their supplies across the Carrying Place. Young Willett, strong as an ox, dragged himself to the encampment at Fort Stanwix, where he collapsed. He lay in a tent desperately ill for two months, his life being despaired of on several occasions. All around him the building of the fort was being carried on, but he saw little of it. He merely lay there, his body wasted to a skeleton. It was early November before he was strong enough to be lifted onto a batteau. He could not lie on deck, because the cold crept into his bones, so he lay on the bottom of the batteau, wrapped in blankets, his weakened body sore from the contact with the rough boards. He was lifted from the batteau at Schenectady and carried overland to Albany, where he remained at the house of a friend until the Hudson River, which had been frozen, broke up sufficiently for him to be taken to New York.

It was a sad home-coming. The news had reached New York that Isaac, the brother who was serving on a British privateer, had been lost at sea. He left a wife and four small children.

The gay young officer who had left New York in May was but a shadow of his former self, but his spirit had not been quenched. As his strength returned he asked to re-enlist, but Edward Willett vetoed the notion and Marinus Willett had fought his last battle for the British.

Son of Liberty

STIRRING EVENTS LAY AHEAD for Marinus Willett but he was not aware of them. His mind was focused on those two problems which present themselves to every man of nineteen, learning a trade and seeking a mate. Marinus possessed little schooling and books held no charm for him. He lived a life that was chiefly physical. Now that Wolfe had taken Quebec at the cost of his own life, the war with France dwindled to a close. Willett found no military service in which he could participate, so he settled down to earning a living with his hands. At the cabinet-maker's shop where he was employed he became attracted to Mary Pearsee, daughter of his employer. They were married, after a brief courtship, at Trinity Church in 1760. A child was born the next year, a boy who was named after his father.

Under ordinary circumstances Willett might have become a New York tradesman, happy with his wife and son, satisfied to earn a living and to hope for financial success. But history plays queer jokes on human beings. And Willett reached maturity in an era when no man could live his own life or do business as usual. Destiny had taken control of America. Events would shape the lives of men, stirring events to which every loyal colonist would relinquish his own interests, even his life, if necessary. Willett, working at his trade, began to realize the vision which George Washington had seen so clearly as he rode through the streets of New York on his spirited horse.

Years before, during the crisis brought about by the Zenger trial involving freedom of the press, a young lawyer, John Morin Scott, had organized the Sons of Liberty. The French War had unified the colonies and the mother country. There had been no need for the Sons of Liberty, who had dissolved. But payment for the war was now an issue in England. Large land-owners, overburdened with taxation, insisted that the colonies share the cost of the victory over France. Pressure was put on Parliament, which passed the Stamp Act in 1765.

Scott, now a prosperous lawyer in New York, expressed his sentiments in the *New York Gazette and Weekly Postboy*, a newspaper owned and edited by John Holt.

"The great fundamental principles of government should be common to all its parts and members, else the whole will be endangered. If, then, the interest of the mother country and her colonies cannot be made to coincide; if the same constitution may not take place in both; if the welfare of the mother country necessarily requires a sacrifice of the most natural rights of the colonies—their right of making their own laws, and disposing of their own property by representatives of their own choosing—if such is really the case between Great Britain and her colonies, *then the connexion between them OUGHT TO CEASE; and, sooner or later, it must inevitably cease.*"

Traitorous words, said Edward Willett, that loyal supporter of George III. His son did not agree. Marinus had witnessed British cruelty at the Fly Market. He had been close to British arrogance and stupidity in the war against the French. He drank in Scott's words, finding them invigorating. He clashed openly with his father, who had retired to Jamaica on Long Island, a spot more congenial than New York to a man with Loyalist sympathies. Marinus relinquished his pew in Trinity Church because the prayers included the names of the King and the royal family and cast his lot with the Presbyterians, considered heretics by the Episcopalians. And he joined the Sons of Liberty, where he met Alexander McDougall, Isaac Sears and John Lamb, all men of action. Mere words would not bring liberty to the colonies. Deeds spoke louder to them. But within the group theory and action were united "like the snow of Jehovah and of Gideon." Common enemies were the government and its officers and those citizens whose timidity or personal interests induced them to act in a subservient manner toward the crown.

In July four fishermen were impressed by the British and carried aboard a ship in the harbor. When the captain came ashore the Sons of Liberty seized him and bore him in triumph to The Fields, their gathering place on the outskirts of the city. The terrified captain agreed to release the prisoners, so a group of patriots went aboard his ship and brought back the fishermen. The captain's barge was burned at the wharf. The city magistrates, unable to fasten the blame on any one individual, fumed with wrath.

The Stamp Act went into effect on November first. Marinus Willett and John Lamb spent the day before printing placards for distribution throughout the city. Holt's newspaper printed "A Funeral Lamentation on the DEATH of LIBERTY who finally expires on this 31st of October in the year of our Lord MDCCLXV and of our Slavery."

The stamps were landed and stored in Lieutenant Governor Cadwallader Colden's house at Fort George. Mysterious placards appeared during the day, urging people to gather at The Fields. Soon after sunset Sears and Willett marched their company of Sons of Liberty to the gathering place, where they erected a gallows on which was suspended an effigy of Colden with a stamped paper in his hand, a drum at his back and a label on his breast bearing the inscription "The Rebel Drummer." By his side hung an effigy of the Devil with a boot in his hand, a satire on the Earl of Bute, at whose instigation the people believed Colden had acted.

Meanwhile a second party had been parading the streets, bearing an effigy of Colden seated in the Lieutenant Governor's own coach, which the Sons of Liberty had appropriated for the occasion. The two groups met at The Fields and marched down Broadway to the fort. The ramparts were lined with soldiers in scarlet coats. Guns loaded with grapeshot frowned from the apertures. Undaunted, the marchers dodged beneath the cannon, knocked with their clubs against the gate and dared Colden to give the order to fire. They also hurled taunts at Major James, who had made the remark that he would ram the stamps down the throats of the rebels with the point of his sword.

The mob surged out of control of its leaders. Bowling Green was stripped of its palisades. The gibbet and its effigies were planted in the circular plot near the fort. Colden's coach, two sleighs and stable fixtures from his barn were piled around the effigies. The whole was set afire, while thousands of throats roared approval.

A group of the most radical Sons of Liberty rushed to Major James' house in the Vauxhall, where they broke in the doors, destroyed the furniture, drank the major's liquor, ransacked the gardens and left the house a mere shell. Exhausted and tipsy, they broke up and went home. At two in the morning the city lay quiet as a tomb.

Marinus Willett won his spurs in this action. From that night he was a recognized leader of that branch of the Sons of Liberty which advocated action regardless of consequences. He made his choice willingly, knowing that his decision might mean the loss of family ties, the sacrifice of his own business future, even death itself.

Governor Moore arrived from England a few days later and won the gratitude of the populace by leaving the obnoxious stamps in possession of the Mayor. And in the following spring, after the repeal of the Stamp Act, the King's birthday was celebrated in The Fields. An ox was roasted whole. A pole was erected, about which were piled twenty-five cords of wood and a dozen tar-barrels. As the fire mounted to the sky, a salute was fired from Fort George and the royal standard was raised to the cheers of the multitude. The crowning achievement of the day was the planting of a Liberty Pole inscribed "The King, Pitt and Liberty."

Three years of peace followed. Marinus Willett, in business with his father-in-law at the Sign of the Clothes Press, located at the upper end of Maiden Lane near the Oswego Market, was advertising desks, breakfast and dining tables, bureaus and a lady's dressing chest and bookcase. He also was doing business as a public auctioneer. At his home in Queens Street, young Marinus, a fine youngster of nine, was preparing to enter King's College, where he hoped to study medicine. It again appeared that Willett was destined for an uneventful business career in New York.

Boston upset the applecart. Opposition of radicals there to British policy had brought an army from Halifax. In September, 1769 Governor Moore died, leaving Colden in charge of New York. When the Assembly voted supplies to the King's troops, the Sons of Liberty rose in revolt. At a gathering in The Fields they defied the act of the Assembly. Alexander McDougall wrote a fiery denunciation of the government and got tossed into jail for his pains. He had so many visitors that he had to issue tickets of admission to his cell. The soldiers destroyed the Liberty Pole and piled it on the steps of a tavern-keeper who was friendly to the Sons of Liberty.

Lamb and Willett again helped to print placards. A meeting was held in The Fields. There was no demonstration, only quiet resistance. The next day Sears and some friends intercepted British soldiers with placards they had intended to nail on doors of citizens. A scuffle ensued. Twenty soldiers came on the run, also some unarmed citizens.

Marinus Willett heard the news at his shop, so he ran through the streets toward Golden Hill, where he found the British soldiers standing off a mob of irate citizens armed with sticks and clubs. A man dressed in an officer's uniform appeared and encouraged the soldiers, who rushed the citizens with fixed bayonets. Willett threw himself into the melee which followed. There was no organization. Each man inflicted what punishment he could. A sailor leading the citizens was cut down. A boy got knocked over the head as he sought refuge in a nearby house. Several soldiers received wounds. Some were disarmed. British officers arrived and ordered the soldiers to their barracks. The mob opened up and let the Britishers pass through. The first battle of the American Revolution had been a victory for the Sons of Liberty. The date, January 18, 1770.

A second Liberty Pole was erected and the Sons of Liberty celebrated their triumph by a banquet and a visit to the jail, where they saluted McDougall with forty-five cheers.

Another lull followed the victory at Golden Hill, but the storm which broke in the spring of 1774 did not cease until American liberty had been established. Taxation without representation was again a cause of the outburst. The tax on tea had already resulted in a Tea Party in Boston. Charleston had refused to accept its quota from the British East India Company. And the Sons of Liberty in New York eagerly awaited the first appearance of a tea ship in the harbor. When it arrived off Sandy Hook on April 18, Captain Lockyer's cargo was refused by the consignee. The captain, who had taken quarters at the Coffee House, was brought to the balcony, greeted with ironic cheers, and later escorted to his ship and wished a pleasant journey home. In The Fields a young King's College student named Alexander Hamilton made his maiden speech in denunciation of the Boston Port

Bill. Committees were appointed to enforce a boycott on British goods. Committees of Correspondence relayed news from colony to colony.

These were uncertain days in the Willett household. Edward Willett was living in Jamaica, completely estranged from his son. Several relatives had come out boldly for the Loyalist cause. Marinus was struggling to make ends meet. His customers had been wealthy merchants and landowners. Many of them were disgusted with his devotion to the Sons of Liberty. His business dwindled now that he had lost his market for fine cabinet-making. And young Marinus, a chip off the old block, was causing trouble for Dr. Myles Cooper at King's College. *The Black Book, or Book of Misdemeanors,* became dotted with complaints against this offshoot of the prominent Son of Liberty. The boy neglected his Latin exercises. With a group of four he stole a large quantity of wine from the president's garret. He was confined within college walls until he made up his translations from Lucian. He broke that confinement, having slipped over the wall at night, probably to witness some demonstration in The Fields. He was ordered to finish his Lucian assignment, also to translate half of the eighth book of Virgil's *Aeneid* into English by the first day of the next term. Young Marinus was evidently more interested in the stirring events surrounding him, for he failed to complete the assignments and was degraded until he completed double of every task he owed.

The boy got his assignments in under the wire, but he had little to fear from Dr. Cooper. The president of King's College had been an open-mouthed adherent to the Loyalist cause. The Sons of Liberty marched to his house one evening. Alexander Hamilton harangued the mob from the steps of the president's residence while Dr. Cooper escaped through the back door. He departed for England a few days later, never to return.

The Sons of Liberty spent an active spring. The boycott

was difficult to enforce, for New York merchants resented any interference with what they considered their right to trade. Some of them were suspected of selling boards to the British to be sent to build barracks for the troops in Boston. The Sons of Liberty boarded the British sloop bound for Boston and took off the boards together with a quantity of straw destined for the British garrison. The next day Isaac Sears was arrested and taken before the Mayor. He refused bail and was sentenced to jail, but Willett and a party attacked the constables and rescued their "King" before he could be imprisoned.

Two days later, in the dusk of a spring evening, a dust-stained horseman rode into the city with the news of the British attempt to seize the American stores at Concord. The fields of Massachusetts had been stained with patriot blood. The preliminaries were over. The British called it open rebellion. To the Sons of Liberty it was war to the death.

The British force was planning to evacuate New York. The Committee agreed to allow them to depart for Boston with their arms and accoutrements. The troops marched from their barracks at ten in the morning of a fine June day. Marinus Willett was talking with friends at a public house in Beekman Slip when a messenger rushed up to him with the information that the soldiers were taking not only their arms, but several carts loaded with arms and ammunition. Willett had been opposed to letting the troops depart at all, for he had been of the opinion that the small British force could be captured without difficulty. He sprang into action. His route led past the Coffee House, where he stopped to give public notice that he was planning to intercept the British ammunition train. He hurried along Water Street to the Exchange. A long procession of carts protected by British soldiers was coming down Broad Street. The first cart had reached the corner of Beaver Street when Willett came running up. The cart was piled high with chests of arms.

Marinus Willett, standing with legs apart in the middle of the intersection, blocked the way. Though he was one man against a British detachment, he seized the bridle of the lead-horse. The cart drew up short, causing an abrupt halt in the procession. A British major, resplendant in scarlet and gold, rode up. Anger had painted his face the same color as his uniform.

"What is the meaning of this insolence?" he asked, placing his hand on his sword. Citizens were gathering from all sides.

Willett's reply was prompt. "The Committee granted you permission to leave the city unmolested, but they gave you no right to take with you spare arms."

A heated argument ensued. The British major ordered Willett to step aside but the lanky cabinet-maker refused to relinquish his hold on the horse's bridle.

Mayor Matthews pushed his way through the crowd. To him the major raised a protest.

The Mayor turned to Willett and said, "I am surprised that you would hazard the peace and endanger the lives of our citizens when you know that the Committee have directed that the troops shall be permitted to depart unmolested."

Willett stared him down. To the Sons of Liberty the Mayor was a Tory. "My Mayor," he said, "the Committee has not authorized the troops to carry off any spare arms. You seem to forget, Sir, that there has been bloody business in Massachusetts recently. The Sons of Liberty are bound together by the ties of honor as well as interest. We are detaining these arms for the use of our country."

Governeur Morris rushed up to see what the trouble might be. The Sons of Liberty had counted on him. To Willett's surprise Morris agreed with the Mayor. Disappointed but not undaunted, Willett argued with Morris.

A throng pressed in on every side, taking sides in the argument. Through it pressed a dignified figure. "It's Mr. Scott," shouted a citizen. "Let Mr. Scott decide."

John Morin Scott listened to arguments from both sides, his keen eyes focused on each speaker in turn, his graying locks shining in the bright sunlight. His decision was final. "Mr. Willett is right," he said. "The Committee have not given the British permission to carry off any spare arms."

Willett jumped to the cart and appealed to the British soldiers. "Here is your chance, men," he cried. "You must feel repugnance at the thought of shedding the blood of men who are devoted to the cause of liberty. You are the tools of a despot. Come over to our side. Enjoy the air of freedom."

An Irishman stepped out of the British ranks and marched forward. Willett pulled him up to his side, while the crowd rent the air with huzzahs. Willett pushed the driver to the ground, seized the reins, turned the horse and cart around, and proceeded back up Beaver Street. The whole procession followed, accompanied by shouting citizens. Pointed taunts were thrown at the crest-fallen soldiers, who were marching in the opposite direction minus the arms and ammunition they had planned to take to Boston. The stores were deposited in a large yard belonging to Abraham Van Dyck, a good Whig who kept an inn on John Street.

II

PARADE

1775 — 1783

On to Quebec!

THE PROVINCIAL CONGRESS decided to strike back at the British by sending an expedition to Canada. One army would march with General Benedict Arnold through Maine. Generals Richard Montgomery and Philip Schuyler were to take the wilderness route through Lakes George and Champlain, capture Montreal and join Arnold's forces in an assault on Quebec. The colony of New York was asked to raise four regiments, each to consist of ten companies of seventy-two men, rank and file, four sergeants, a drum and fife, in command of a captain and two lieutenants. The city of New York was to furnish one of these regiments. Alexander McDougall, that fiery Son of Liberty, was given the command, with the rank of colonel. The lieutenant colonel, Adolph Ritzema, hardly an ardent patriot, was the son of a prominent Dutch minister. Sedwitz, the major, was chosen because of his experience as an officer in the Swiss army.

Marinus Willett received his appointment as captain in June. The commission was conditional on his ability to raise sufficient recruits to fill a company. Other captains were those staunch Sons of Liberty, William Goforth, Robert Varick, Gershom Mott, Samuel Broome and James Cheeseman. A Prussian veteran, Frederick Weissenfelt, also led a company. Goforth and Willett drilled their men at Abraham Van Dyck's tavern. Long advertisements were inserted in the patriotic *New York Journal*, promising recruits that "from the time of their inlistment, to enter into immediate pay, at one shilling and eleven pence per day; and also to receive one dollar per week, until they are encamped, in order to enable them to support themselves in the intermediate time; and they are likewise to be provided with a suit of regimental clothes, a firelock, ammunition, accoutrements, and every other article necessary for the equipment of AMERICAN SOLDIERS. GOD save the CONGRESSES." The recruiting officers had orders to enlist no deserters from the ministerial army, no stroller, Negro or vagabond or person suspected of being an enemy to the liberty of America, nor under eighteen years of age. On July 18 Congress made the age limits 16 to 50.

Recruiting offered no difficulty, the chief problem being one of selection. At a time when two governments were struggling for control of the city, it took considerable discernment to single out recruits loyal to the patriotic cause. The Sons of Liberty knew how to sift the wheat from the chaff.

On Tuesday, August 15 the first division of McDougall's battalion of provincials sailed to join General Philip Schuyler at Fort Ticonderoga. Ritzema was in command and Willett's company was with his outfit. The soldiers were poorly equipped as to clothing, for the promised regimentals had not been obtainable. But there was no lack of fighting equipment. Hadn't the Sons of Liberty secured quantities of muskets and ammunition in their raid on the arsenal? Hadn't Marinus Willett captured the British ammunition train? British equipment was excellent and American hands had been trained to use it.

Schuyler, in command of the Northern Department, found his task beset with obstacles. He didn't know whether he could move the troops from New York without the consent of Congress. Ready money was non-existent in the colony. He borrowed £20,000 from Governor Trumbull of Connecticut to help finance the expedition. He also purchased

100 head of cattle from Connecticut farmers, with orders to have them driven over to the Hudson River.

At Albany he received news from Fort Ticonderoga that one barrel of flour remained at the fort. A dispute raged among the officers. The living quarters were filthy and inadequate. Schuyler rode to Ticonderoga, where he found all his expectations realized. "I have neither Boats sufficient nor any materials prepared for Building them," he wrote to General Washington. "The stores I ordered from New York are not yet arrived; I have therefore not a Nail, No Pitch, no Oakham, and want a variety of articles indispensably necessary . . . No powder has come, not a gun carriage, very little provision." The Green Mountain Boys were still arguing over who should lead them. "The troops here are destitute of Tents, they are crowded in Vile Barracks, Which with the natural Inattention of the Soldiery to Cleanliness, has already been productive of Desease and numbers are daily rendered unfit for Duty."

Schuyler, in bad health, was called to Saratoga to visit the bedside of his wife and remained there until she was out of danger. While there he saw Colonel Ritzema and the New Yorkers pass through on their way to Ticonderoga. General Montgomery had reviewed them the day before and had passed favorably upon their appearance and training. Maybe the bile inside Schuyler made him feel irritable, for he wrote that though Ritzema's detachment of four companies had a quantity of baggage sufficient for three complete regiments, he had already lost fourteen men through desertion. In Schuyler's opinion he was destined to lose more before he reached Ticonderoga but, he added, "If those gone are like some remaining, we have gained by their going off."

The New Yorkers embarked for Crown Point on Monday, August 28th at six in the evening. The Connecticut troops went with them. General Montgomery was in command. Youthful, energetic and ambitious, this ill-fated officer was impatient to be on the move, but a downpour of rain and the night's blackness forced the party to land. The men spent the night in the woods without tents. They reached Crown Point the following day.

On Wednesday 1200 men embarked in batteaux, escorted by an armed sloop, six schooners and two row-galleys. Their destination was the Isle aux Noix near the entrance to the Sorel River. Here they planned to stop the enemy's vessels by pickets and booms until the main army could bring up some artillery.

The first attempt upon Fort St. John's was made on September 6th. The Continentals were filled with enthusiasm. These hearty American lads would not turn their noses from the smell of gunpowder. Marinus Willett, after his experience under Abercrombie, was not so sure. He had seen British regulars run when attacked from ambush. Some of Johnson's Iroquois were with the defenders of Fort St. John's. News had come through that an American's scalped head dripped blood from a pole in front of the fort. The men laughed off this rumor. They were city lads, unfamiliar with the code of the wilderness. But Willett had not erased from his memory the ghastliness of those first scalpings he had witnessed in the French War.

The batteaux landed a mile and a half from the fort. The men, impetuous and enthusiastic, could hardly wait to advance. Willett and the other officers scurried to and fro, cursing and pleading, but no order resulted. A slipshod advance was made toward the forest, from which a line of fire suddenly spurted. Men began to fall. Some returned the fire. Others fled toward the batteaux. It was hopeless to try to organize them. A camp was made on the shore. The reckoning showed six men killed or wounded. It was reported that the enemy, who had fled after the skirmish, had suffered similar losses. The batteaux rowed back to the Isle aux Noix.

Montgomery was boiling. The men were disgruntled. Several were caught while trying to desert and were subjected to Moses' law of thirty-nine lashes on the bare back. Others were pleading illness and asking to go home on furlough. A Captain Doolittle of Connecticut and Lieutenant John Quackenbush of New York, whom Willett termed "an overgrown bull calf," were granted leaves by Montgomery.

Willett remarked to the general that the ranks were thinning fast.

"Yes," replied Montgomery. "When we get rid of the Do Littles and the Quakes in the Bush I hope we shall have none left but fighting men on whom I can rely."

Fortunately, provisions were ample, so four days later a well-fed army, better organized now that it had had a taste of battle, landed at the spot of the initial failure. Captain Willett was detached with Colonel Ritzema's group of 500 men to take a post below the fort to cut off supplies from the enemy. They had gone but a short distance along a narrow path when the woods began to blaze fire. Indian whoops shrilled through the air. Willett, accustomed to this method of fighting, yelled for his men to drown out the Indians with their own shouts, but the tongues of the recruits clung to dry mouths. Ritzema, the Dutchman of uncertain affections, ordered a retreat which became a pell-mell rout through the woods. The men arrived on shore to find Montgomery's whole army in confusion. Two enemy batteaux mounted with twelve-pounders had fired with deadly effect into the American ranks. A reply from Montgomery's cannon had struck one of the batteaux amidships, sinking it with thirty-five men. The Americans cheer was short-lived. Sailing down the river in all their majesty appeared the two 180-ton warships which had been launched at St. John's. The Americans jumped into their batteaux and fled post-haste to the Isle aux Noix.

Rain fell for three days, cold, chilling rain. Schuyler, succumbing to his pains, retreated to Ticonderoga in a covered batteau, leaving Montgomery in command. That general was disgusted with affairs. A large American army had been routed by two warships and two batteaux. More men were arriving, cursing the rain. The Americans landed for a third time. It was mortifying to Willett that another detachment was sent to complete the circling movement which Ritzema had failed to accomplish. With his customary tendency to jump at conclusions, Willett decided that the Dutch colonel was not only a coward but a traitor. It took two years for the army to find that out. Ritzema was drummed out of the service and joined the enemy forces.

Willett did not know that among the men sent to perform the circling movement was one Peter Gansevoort. The party had been forced to camp in a marsh over night. Young Gansevoort had come down with a fever which incapacitated him, but the Albany Dutchman had insisted that he accompany Montgomery to Montreal. He was carried with the army on a stretcher.

Captain Willett was assigned to the less interesting task of erecting batteries for Lamb's New York artillery. Two batteries were completed, one between 800 and 900 yards from Fort St. John's, the other in the woods 600 yards from the fortifications. These operations were carried on under enemy fire. Because of a scarcity of ammunition the Americans were unable to return the fire; they suffered a loss of five men killed and wounded. It wasn't until Captain John Lamb came up with his artillery company that the Americans were able to exchange shot for shot with the enemy.

One piece of good news came in. Major Brown of Massachusetts had taken Chambly, a smaller fortification twelve miles down the Sorel River. He had brought in a quantity of military stores, including 124 barrels of powder and over 6000 musket cartridges, articles essential to the American cause.

Montgomery sent for Marinus Willett. He had already dispatched a courier to Ticonderoga to inform Schuyler of Brown's victory. Willett was ordered to take the British prisoners to Ticonderoga, and return immediately. Willett, disappointed, gathered the redcoats, put them in batteaux and had them rowed down the lake. He arrived at Ticonderoga at five in the afternoon and turned over his prisoners. He wished to go right back, for he wished to be in at the surrender of St. John's, but his men thought otherwise; they preferred to rest a day or two before returning. Willett stared at them. He noticed their drawn faces and saw that their clothes hardly covered their nakedness. He waited at Ticonderoga for two days.

In the meantime St. John's had capitulated. The British garrison had held out manfully, despite a heavy bombardment from the investing forces. General Carleton, marching to the relief of the fort, was tossed back by Lieutenant Colonel Warren. The garrison, short of food, could hold out no longer. A drum sounded the chamade and a flag appeared from the fort. Two officers were brought blind-folded to Montgomery's tent. They signed the articles of capitulation. The garrison of 600 marched out of the fort and grounded their arms, while the Americans took possession of the last obstacle between them and Montreal.

Willett reached St. John's to discover that the army had already marched. He arrived at Montreal on November 22 to find that the main army had entered the city nearly a week before. General Arnold, after struggling through the Maine wilderness, was outside Quebec awaiting reinforcements from Montgomery before attacking that city. The glory which Marinus Willett craved was to come to him at last. Despite the bitter cold and the snow which covered the desolate landscape, his heart beat warm with anticipation of deeds to be performed, glorious deeds dear to the heart of a soldier.

A day or two later he was on his way back through the French settlements. Montgomery had assigned him to command Ft. St. John's. Willett took the assignment in stride, though the blow must have been terrific. His enlistment would run out in January, when he would go back to Montgomery and plead for a better post.

St. John's, now that the British had been driven back to Canada, was a relatively unimportant post, but it had significance for Willett. For the first time he was actually in command of a company of 54 men with no superior officer nearer than Ticonderoga. On October 30th he wrote to General Schuyler. Montgomery had ordered him to St. John's with instructions "to put the buildings in as good repair as the Season of the Year would admit off. This I shall endeavour to do in the best manner I can, but am doubtfull after I have done my best it will be but an uncomfortable place to Winter in."

Willett faced the problem of handling parties that were daily passing through to Canada. Wounded and prisoners were being sent back to Albany. Provisions were sorely needed. "I am apprehensive the Flower we have here . . . will not be sufficient for the supplys of the garrison," he wrote to Schuyler, "nor is there any Butter at all in this Garrison."

The weather turned cold and snowy and the fort was ill-suited to house the garrison comfortably. The men became discontented, even unruly. One private, being especially troublesome, was sent to Ticonderoga with a recommendation from Willett that he be discharged.

By the end of January Willett was back in Montreal, pleading to be sent to Quebec. But hadn't he performed his task of escorting prisoners well? He was sent down once more, this time in sleighs, with British officers and their families in his charge. He dumped them unceremoniously at Albany and rode horseback to New York, where he arrived on the evening of March 5, 1776.

He was downhearted, to say the least. He had gone forth

charged with enthusiasm, visions of glory filling his mind. He had done every assigned task well. And he was being rewarded by continual retreats. Escorting prisoners! What a task for a man who loved the smell of gunpowder!

Though Willett did not know it, young Peter Gansevoort was feeling much the same way. After going through the hardships of the trip to Montreal in a litter, he had been refused permission to march on to Quebec until after the assault had been made and General Montgomery, critically wounded, had been dragged through the snow by that upstart, Colonel Aaron Burr. Then he had been promoted to lieutenant colonel, though he never understood why, and had been assigned to command the unimportant post at Fort George.

At Ticonderoga a man had kept his eyes and ears open, despite the fact that ill health had prevented him from active participation in the campaign. Philip Schuyler knew Gansevoort well. He also was intimate with the Van Schaicks and wasn't Peter engaged to young Catherine? He had learned of Peter's insistence upon accompanying the expedition to Canada despite the fact that the young man was lying ill with fever.

Schuyler had also been watching the lanky New Yorker, Marinus Willett. Years later Schuyler wrote to Governor George Clinton: "As to Colo. Willett, I conceived very early In this war that he was an Excellent Officer. Indeed I give myself some credit for the opinion I formed of him in 1775 as he had on every occasion evinced that It was a just one." Much to Willett's surprise and pleasure his commission as major came through from the Provincial Congress in April. A sick man in Albany had been pulling the strings.

Dark Days

HYSTERIA HAD STRUCK NEW YORK. General Washington had been forced out of Boston. Hostile sails might appear off Sandy Hook at any moment. Workmen labored day and night on fortifications being thrown up along the spine of Manhattan Island. The streets were gay with marching militia—the Fusiliers, the Corsicans, the Bold Foresters and the Oswego Rangers—all arrayed in multi-colored uniforms.

Marinus Willett, busy enlisting men for a company in the new Fourth New York regiment, looked down his nose at these "society soldiers." Young New Yorkers did not, with the result that Willett, after months of labor, enlisted but 18 men, while the gaily-uniformed militia had waiting lists.

Willett, fearful that his inability to enlist a company might lead to his dismissal, wrote to John Jay and sent him Schuyler's letter of recommendation.

Jay's reply did not contain much encouragement. "The subject of your letter deserves attention; it is however unnecessary for me to repeat what I have already said relative to it, except again to assure you that my endeavours shall not be wanting to obtain for you an appointment equal to your merit. General Schuyler's letter does you honor and had it been made known to the members of Congress a few months sooner, I am confident it would have had all the influence you would have wished."

The blow fell on May 9, scarcely two weeks after Willett

had received Jay's answer. Captains Brown and Willett of McDougall's regiment were dismissed from the service "not from any dissatisfaction with their conduct, but with great reluctance from necessity only because they have been so unfortunate in their attempts to recruit their companies."

Willett had friends in the Provincial Congress. On April 27 he was recommended for the office of major in the Fourth New York regiment, but evidently did not receive the appointment.

General Washington entered New York that same day at the head of the Continental Army. His presence lent encouragement to the efforts of the citizens. Marinus Willett could not be kept out of action. He swallowed considerable pride before he joined Colonel John Lasher's militia, but join he did, and set to work building the Bayard's Hill redoubt west of the Bowery.

The Tories on Long Island were worrying the Provincial Congress. Attempts to disarm Loyalists in Jamaica and Hempstead added flame to the conflict. Lord Stirling and Charles Lee both tried to suppress revolts and Isaac Sears entered Newtown and forced the oath of allegiance on 400 Tories. Over in Jamaica Edward Willett swallowed the oath "as if it were a four-pound shot." Congress ordered the enrollment of all residents of Long Island capable of bearing arms. Captain Richard Hewlett, leader of the Tories, threatened to "warm the pants" of any party sent to disarm him. John Morin Scott trailed the Tories to De Moth's swamp, where that innkeeper hung out a white flag to warn against the approaching militia.

Hewlett continued to defy Congress. Mayor Matthews of New York, now a Tory refugee at Jamaica, joined with him in a plot to kidnap Washington.

Colonel Lasher, aware that Willett had been brought up in Jamaica, assigned him the task of routing out the conspirators, who had fortified a hill outside Jamaica.

Willett's party took the road to Jamaica at a canter. The fields lay wide and green, scarcely disturbed by the slight breeze from the Sound. The attractive houses, set at a distance from the road, were strangely silent. Willett, riding at the head of his troop, made a mental note of the names associated with the Loyalist cause—Hicks, Hewitt, Polhemus, Willett.

He halted the troop before the courthouse, where he learned that the Tories on the fortified hill were prepared to sell their lives at the dearest price. He knew the terrain, so he planned his attack carefully. Cavalry would be useless. This fight would have to enlist Indian methods, so he dismounted his horsemen and arranged them in a circle which would close in as it climbed the hill. The men were ordered to dodge from tree to tree and to withhold fire until he gave the signal.

The party started forward slowly, cautiously. Each tree became a temporary shelter. Not a rifle was fired. A Tory head appeared above the rudely constructed barricade and a shot shattered the air.

Willett gave the order to fire and a brisk exchange ensued. The Tories, surrounded and outnumbered, signalled their willingness to surrender. One had been killed and several wounded. Eighteen were rounded up and taken to New York. Edward Willett was not among them. The shutters of his house were closed as the troop rode by. Willett did not stop to make inquiries. This was no time for reconciliation.

Such duties in the field suited Willett but they did not provide food for himself and family. He had not received a cent for his service in the Canadian campaign. His business, which had suffered during his absence, was a complete ruin. Something had to be done to earn money.

The opportunity came in June. Willett had dropped in at the Coffee House, where he ran into Peter Simm, a friend noted for his crack-pot schemes. This time Simm had come up with a dandy. With the financial aid of two friends, he planned to set up furnaces on Long Island for the purpose of extracting salt from sea water.

Willett fell in with Simm's scheme. They petitioned Congress for £1000, one half to be lent in advance without interest for 1½ years. Without waiting for Congressional action the men set to work on their project, Willett's job being to transport materials from Hell Gate and Staten Island to Huntington and Cold Spring, where Simm began to erect the furnace.

These were eventful days in New York. Much progress had been made on the fortifications. Over in Brooklyn preparations were being completed for the defense of Long Island. And on the 9th of July the Declaration of Independence was read to the combined American armies in The Fields. Marinus Willett stood at the head of his company of militia, his eyes focused on the face of General Washington, his ears tuned to the words of Thomas Jefferson. The break had come. Now all patriots knew for what they were fighting. It was war to a finish.

The British fleet sailed into the harbor a few days later. Sailors landed on Long Island. Among other deeds they destroyed the salt works upon which Peter Simm had pinned not his own hopes but those of Marinus Willett.

The battle of Long Island was fought in August. General John Sullivan, after suffering defeat at the hands of the British, was captured. The militia fled in headlong rout toward the shore. If they could be carried across the Sound to Manhattan, the army might be saved to fight again.

Alexander McDougall took charge of the boats and Willett worked with him. The crossings started in the evening; there were rowboats, whaleboats, flatboats, sloops and sailboats, for McDougall had requisitioned everything that would float and some that would not. Things went badly from the start. The militiamen, completely panic-stricken, rushed down the slopes and crowded the beach. Men fought with one another for places in the boats. Even the elements aligned themselves against McDougall and Willett. A northeaster sprang up. Rain deluged the weary troops. The tide became unfavorable. Nothing could be done with the sloops in an adverse wind. It would be impossible to save the militia if only rowboats were used. McDougall sent a messenger to inform General Washington of the danger, but he could not be found. The work went on, doggedly but without hope.

At eleven the wind shifted and the rain ceased. Washington appeared, calm, cool, efficient. Probably the American leader never shone more magnificently than at this desperate moment. The boats moved across the Sound, which had become smooth as glass. Some of them were loaded so heavily that their gunwales touched the water. All was orderly now. The shattered New Jersey and New Hampshire troops crawled into the boats, dragging their wounded with them. At last the gallant band of Marylanders, having protected the retreat at a cost that was appalling, staggered to the beach for their hard-earned ride across the Sound. The darkest day of the Revolution was over.

Mary Willett had lingered in the city, hoping against hope that the British would be repulsed. Young Marinus, who had taken part in the battle, got back safely, though smeared with mud and completely exhausted. When his mother packed up the few belongings that a wagon would hold and set out for Danbury, Connecticut, the boy insisted upon staying in the city to fight beside his father.

New York was not relinquished without a struggle. At Harlem Heights the retreating Continentals and militia raised havoc with the redcoats, but the tired, poorly-equipped Americans at last retreated beyond White Plains, while the British took possession of New York. They were not to give it up for seven years.

Young Marinus enlisted as surgeon's mate under Dr. Mc-

Knight of New York and joined the main army near White Plains. His father busied himself supplying the army with food and ammunition, much of which he smuggled from Long Island to the Connecticut ports and transported overland to White Plains. He had applied for a commission as lieutenant colonel in Colonel Peter Gansevoort's Third New York regiment.

The commission arrived in November and on the 24th Willett wrote the following letter of acceptance to Robert Yates, Chairman of the Committee of Arrangements at Fishkill: "I have received your account of my appointment by the Committe of arrangement for the State of New York, who you inform me have pleased to take notice of my former Rank and Services. I can by no means think of refusing to attend to the Voice of my Countrey at so Critical and important a Period as this. I shall therefore with cheerfullness receive the appointment with which I am honoured, nor shall my best endeavours be wanting to render to my country every service I am capable.

"Some business I have undertaken for the Quarter Master Generall of the Continental Armey has engaged my attendance at North Castle tomorrow, after which I shall immediately attend the Committee of Arrangement at the Fish-kill, and am in the meantime with sincere respect, Sir. your most obedient Humble servant."

The Hudson

THE WINTER OF 1776-1777 found Lieutenant Colonel Willett at Fishkill recruiting and drilling men for the Third New York regiment. Gansevoort, ten years younger than Willett, and madly in love with Catherine, sister of Colonel Goose Van Schaick, was enlisting men in Albany. Upon Willett devolved the task of disciplining a regiment, a thankless job for which his talents were peculiarly adapted. A disciplinarian at heart, the lanky, hawk-nosed colonel faced his problem with determination and efficiency. Enlistments were for brief periods, often for three months. Bounties were paid to soldiers who offered their services, a procedure ideally suited to the shrewdness of the Yankee mind, for soldiers found that by enlisting in one regiment, receiving the bounty, then deserting and enrolling in a second regiment, they could make a decent living and acquire warm clothes and a gun for squirrel hunting. To curb this practice General McDougall ordered officers to apprehend these men and have them court-martialled. Whosoever were convicted and sentenced to die might "consider their execution certain and inevitable." To identify recruits, pieces of blue or yellow ribbon or tape were to be sewed on the hat of each man at the time of his enlistment and were not to be removed until the regimental corps to which the recruit was assigned might be assembled. The penalty for failure to wear identification insignia was to be thirty-nine lashes on the bare back.

The recruits were mostly country bumpkins, capable with the plow and expert at squirrel hunting, but careless about their appearance and stupid regarding military procedure. Willett, immaculate in his person and bound round with red tape, insisted that his men be clean and disciplined. He ordered the sergeants to teach the recruits to clean their own firearms and to mount and unmount the firelocks, rather than lean upon a neighbor to do these things for them. Inspections of quarters and of the soldiers' persons and clothing were taken as a matter of course. The men were divided into groups. The inferior and "Extreme Awkward" men were drilled one, two or three at a time "for their uncommon Awkwardness."

Many soldiers were without muskets. Willett, in desperation, wrote to Major General Schuyler on Febraury 18: "Upon applycation to Genll. McDougall for the recruits of Colonel Gansevoort's Regiment who rendezvous at this place, I was directed to write to you to know whether the Regiment is not to be armed at Albany, as he supposes there are plenty of good arms there. As the matter of having the Regiment well armed nearly affects me, I humbly beg your directions about this affair as soon as you conveniently can; observing to you, that besides the chance I have of procuring some good arms at this place if an order can be obtained for that purpose, the advantage or disadvantage of having the recruits driled which depends upon my having or not having arms is no inconsiderable object, nor is the keeping part of the Regiment at this place untill we are ordered to take the field of no account, as by that means we have an eaqual chance with the Regiments about here in recruiting."

Captains were ordered to make returns of their several companies, their arms, accoutrements and clothing, and deliver copies to the adjutant, who was compiling the regimental roll. The companies were to parade according to their superiority, the first company on the right, the second on the left, and so on, placing the youngest troops in the center. The regiment was to hold itself in readiness to march on slightest notice.

Imagine Willett's disappointment when a letter came through in March ordering Colonel Gansevoort and part of the regiment to march up the Mohawk Valley to Fort Stanwix and Willett's detachment was not included. Instead he was assigned to command Fort Constitution, the least important of a string of fortifications guarding the Hudson River. Though the blow was severe, he ordered his men "to cook provisions this evening for tomorrow the Regiment is to march early in the morning. Beating of assembly will be very early. Lieut. Warner to take charge of the teams to carry Regimental baggage and to folow with as much expedition as possible. Lieut. Tapp to remain at Fishkill to forward recruits."

Fort Constitution was located at Martlaer's Island on the east side of the river opposite West Point. Beside the barracks and storehouses, it boasted four batteries. The point of approach up the Hudson was guarded by a battery of eleven guns. On the shore in the center of the island stood two more batteries, one of eight guns, the other fourteen. Between these defenses was a round tower boasting eight guns. Across the river, surmounting the heights, another fort was being built, a large structure which later would be called Fort Arnold, after its commanding officer.

Marinus Willett, after arriving at Fort Constitution, wrote his military creed into his Orderly Book: "As Millatary glory is only to be Obtain'd by firmness The Commanding Officer takes this early Opportunity of recommending Dilligence & unanimity to the Garrison. They may depend upon it that He will make it his Business to have Justice Regularly Administred as without a well Regulated Discipline all the powers of an Army become innervated."

Orders flew fast. Reveille at daybreak. Troop at 9 A.M.

Retreat at sundown. Tattoo at 9 P.M. Sentinels to be numbered and given the sign. Boats passing the fort to be brought to and asked to give an account of themselves. Armorers, artificers, bakers, sutlers, retailers in the garrison to report to the commanding officer immediately. Rooms to be washed every Wednesday and Saturday. All lights out at tattoo. No guns to be fired. No strangers to be admitted to the garrison. Parade Sunday at ten. Countersign—Victory.

Action came quickly, unexpectedly. The garrison was on Sunday parade when a messenger rushed up to Willett with a hastily-scrawled note. McDougall at Peekskill had been attacked by the British. A frigate, four transports and several smaller vessels had appeared early in the morning. A thousand men had been landed. McDougall, with quarter that number, had fought back briefly before setting fire to the mill on Gregory's Creek and retreating to the highlands. The British were burning the barracks and plundering his supply bases. Would Willett come post haste with his garrison? Possibly they might drive the British back to the boats before everything at Peekskill was lost.

Willett found McDougall on the top of a hill overlooking Peekskill. Smoke was rising from the burning barracks. The enemy was hurrying through the countryside, burning and plundering. Willett saw a party of 100 redcoats set fire to a house, which stood on a hill well in advance of the British army. A deep ravine lay between them and McDougall.

Willett took in the situation at a glance. By a quick movement his detachment could gain the enemy's rear and drive them back or cut them off. He suggested the plan to McDougall, but his old friend, reckless with words as a Son of Liberty, was conservative in the field. He dared not attack. He must wait for reinforcements. Willett told him waiting would accomplish nothing. The British would burn the village. McDougall consented.

Willett's party threaded its way through the ravine and

circled to the rear of the British. Falling dusk made the terrain vague and several fences intervened, but Willett gave the order to advance. The Third New Yorkers, a line of gray and green, rushed toward the hill, hurdled the fences, all the while shouting their battle cries to the darkening sky. The British, after a brief encounter, turned tail and ran for their ships, leaving behind them blankets and a few cloaks, welcome articles at Fort Constitution. The prize was a blue camelot cloak which a British officer had tossed aside in his flight. It fell to the lot of Captain Abraham Swartwout, a frugal Dutchmen in Willett's regiment.

The British boarded their ships and sailed down the river. Later they were to boast of their exploit at Peekskill. They had destroyed 500 barrels of flour and 80 hogsheads of rum at the mill on Gregory's Creek. They also had burned the barracks, the magazine, the workshops and storehouses, 150 new wagons, tools, beef, pork, molasses, tallow, nails and part of McDougall's camp equipage. If Willett had not appeared, a worse disaster might have befallen Peekskill. It was the lanky New Yorker's first real exploit and it won for him praises from the patriotic newspapers, one of which wrote: "Colonel Willett having accordingly made the necessary disposition, advanced with his small party with the greatest firmness and resolution and made the attack. The enemy instantly fled with the greatest precipitation, leaving three men dead on the field and the whole body, panic struck, betook themselves to their shipping, embarking under cover of night. McDougall went back to his quarters at Peekskill. Never did troops exhibit more firmness and resolution than did our army on this occasion."

Life at Fort Constitution continued to be disorderly. Soldiers were punished for selling their clothes. There were several courts martial. Willett thanked his lucky stars when a letter arrived from General McDougall dated May 12: "Lieut Col Lorin has marched to relieve you. Whenever he arrives, and takes possession of the Fort, join your regiment as soon as possible. You will send for any of your men, who are near you; and leve direction for the recruiting officers, who are to join you. I wish you a good passage, and march; and may God Protect you and your Corps."

Stanwix Would never Surrender

WILLETT EMBARKED WITH 200 men for Albany, where he visited Catherine Van Schaick and picked up a letter to deliver to her "dear Peter." The detachment marched to Schenectady, from which point they took off after loading seven batteaux with baggage. Major Robert Cochran met Willett's party at Fort Dayton. Cochran, son of the surgeon general, was a dapper chap with small, sensitive features and a broad forehead. He brought news from Fort Stanwix. The Indians were stirring to the north. Sir John Johnson and Colonel John Butler had been active among them. Rumors had come from the friendly Oneidas of an invasion from Oswego some time in the summer. Fort Stanwix, the most isolated outpost on the New York frontier, would be its objective.

Willett mustered his detachment and singled out six officers, forty privates and two drummers to leave at Fort Dayton. Willett asked Cochran to march the rest of the group to Fort Stanwix, while he and Dr. Hunlock Woodruff, surgeon at the fort, rode ahead up the river. They crossed the Mohawk at the fording place near old Fort Schuyler and, after splashing through the shallow waters of Oriskany Creek, reached Stanwix at sundown.

The squat fortifications, bathed in the slanting light from the west, did not look formidable. Willett, stretching his memory back nearly twenty years, remembered the long nights and days when he had lain helpless behind the partly-constructed walls, while General Stanwix and his men carried logs from the forest and set them into place. Willett had never expected to see this fort again, but here he was.

He and Dr. Woodruff passed the ruins of Fort William at the upper landing of the Carrying Place which formed a link between the Mohawk River and Wood Creek. Over this stretch of a mile and a half ran a rude road which led past the main gate of Stanwix toward old Fort Newport. The two men rode up to the fort.

Colonel Peter Gansevoort received "dear Caty's" letter, his florid face wreathed in smiles, his gray eyes shining. The two tall men stood for a long moment, their hands clasped in grips that were strong and friendly, for there was much in common between the cabinet-maker from New York and the Albany Dutchman. Though Willett might be the better disciplinarian, the Dutch colonel performed his duties methodically and could be exacting in emergencies. They each had a softer side. Gansevoort knew that Willett dabbled in poor poetry, while Willett was tolerant of the flair for music which was such an obsession with his superior officer that he had enlisted his teacher in his regiment so that he could continue his studies. Gansevoort, though the officer in command, was willing to relinquish some of his authority to Willett, ten years his senior; and Willett, who might have rankled under the orders of another younger man, never had reason to criticize Gansevoort for that officiousness which characterized sons of wealthy families whose connections had gained them military offices. Beyond everything else the two men were bound together by the one thing which was to bring them fame on the frontier—an intense loyalty to their country.

Yet these two brave men, compatible in most respects, were to lock horns. The point of disagreement was Capt. B. de la Marquisie, a French engineer whom General Schuyler had sent to superintend the remodelling of the fort against the expected invasion from Oswego.

Willett's inspection of the fort roused his ire immediately. Barracks had been completed inside the enclosure and another large and commodious structure to house troops had been built outside the glacis. Willett considered this latter idea preposterous. Who ever heard of barracks outside a fort on an isolated frontier subject to immediate attack by an invading force? In addition de la Marquisie was working the men overtime procuring logs from the swamp. When he began to erect them in the covert-way and not in the center of the ditch where the old palisades had been placed, Willett grew suspicious of the engineer's ability. These pickets were to be placed about three feet from the parapet of the glacis. Two of them were to be framed together as cross pieces to form a kind of port-hole. But why in hell were the logs being cut seventeen feet long, when the pickets were to be only ten? Willett could not understand, unless de la Marquisie had some intention other than engineering ignorance. Willett, always ready to jump at conclusions, rushed to Gansevoort to protest this blundering incompetence or traitorous act or whatever de la Marquisie had in mind. Gansevoort received the protest calmly. He did not believe de la Marquisie incompetent, nor did he see anything traitorous in the French engineer's acts. He would not send de la Marquisie down to Schuyler to be cashiered. Willett, taking matters in his own hands, sat down and wrote a long letter to Schuyler, airing in detail his grievances against de la Marquisie.

The repairs continued, slowly, inexpertly, while the threat from the north became more real. How Stanwix could be defended in its incompleted condition was more than Willett could fathom. He blustered and stormed, to no avail. The showdown came when de la Marquisie began to erect the pickets, which came across the necks of the embrasures. The portholes were not opposite. There was nothing to do but knock off the necks of the embrasures, a long, arduous task. Gansevoort had been seeing things, too, but it was not until July that a letter came from Schuyler, requesting that the French engineer be returned to Albany.

Meanwhile common difficulties forced Willett and Gansevoort to pull together. Indians appeared frequently: their whoops broke the stillness at night; their fleet forms could be seen flitting from tree to tree during the day. Among Willett's officers was Captain James Gregg, well-liked but not too sensitive to duty. Several of his men had come up for court martial, both at Fort Constitution and at Fort Stanwix. Orders had been issued against officers or soldiers straying into the woods outside the clearing.

Gregg, feeling the urge to hunt pigeons, left the fort after breakfast one day in June, accompanied by Corporal Madison of his company. Shortly after three in the afternoon Gregg was carried into the fort. His head was a mass of blood. His body hung limp in the arms of two soldiers. His scalp had been lifted. A bullet had entered his side. Madison, also scalped, was dead. Gregg, still conscious but seemingly near death, told of his ghastly experience He and Madison were shooting pigeons near the river when they heard shots. Gregg fell. An Indian ran toward him, waving a tomahawk. Gregg, feigning death, lay perfectly still. The Indian's knife struck at his forehead and slid expertly around his scalp. A quick tug from above, painful, nauseating, caused Gregg to bite his lips to keep from crying out. He must have fainted, for he awoke with blood running into his eyes and down his face. Madison lay stretched out on his face a few feet away; his head was a liquid red. Gregg dragged himself over to his companion to find Madison dead. Unable to get to his feet, afraid to cry out, he consulted his watch, saw that it was ten o'clock, rested his throbbing head against the body of his friend and awaited his fate. After what seemed eternity to him, two fishermen approached. They had heard Gregg's dog barking and had run to the spot. They brought a relief party from the fort. And here he was. Gregg smiled wanly while Dr. Woodruff dressed his wounds.

Willett was furious. But what could one do to a man who had endured scalping without crying out? Poor brave fool! Let him die in peace. But Gregg refused to die. In three weeks he was sent down to Albany with other wounded men.

The soldiers at Stanwix were an unruly lot. A sergeant was reduced to the ranks for sleeping on post. A private suffered 100 lashes on his bare back for taking a pocketbook with six dollars. Several members of the garrison were tried for drunkenness, and one radical received 100 lashes for cursing Congress and saying that the men would desert.

The first anniversary of the Declaration of Independence was not celebrated at Fort Stanwix. The garrison had too much to do. Scouting parties were out in several directions. A detachment was felling trees to obstruct Wood Creek, which led to Oneida Lake. Another group was repairing the road to Fort Dayton, from which point relief would come. The work on the fortifications was blundering along under the incapable hands of de la Marquisie. And only the day before Ensign Spoor, out on fatigue with 16 privates cutting sods for Fort Newport, had been attacked by Indians. One private had been brought in dead. His body had been unhumanly mangled. Two more men had been wounded. Spoor and six privates were missing. Two relief parties had been unable to contact the enemy. To make matters worse, a run of hot weather had spoiled the beef. Willett had to announce that there were provisions in the fort for only six weeks. It is possible that he and Gansevoort forgot about the anniversary, for, though Gansevoort wrote at length to Schuyler that night, he mentioned no celebration.

July 27th brought two kinds of news. About noon, as Willett lay resting in his bunk after a hard morning at the fortifications, trying desperately to repair the mistakes of the departed de la Marquisie, he heard three guns fired in quick succession. Jumping to his feet, he ran to the parapet. A sentinel was hurrying along the edge of the glacis, closely followed by a girl who staggered along, holding in her hand a small basket. Blood ran down her small breasts, staining her homespun dress. Willett went with a small detachment to a spot near the edge of the clearing, where he gazed down on the bodies of two dead girls, both scalped and mutilated by tomahawks. The three girls had been picking raspberries. One of the dead children was the daughter of an old British artilleryman who had lived at the fort since the French War. Though he had been given chances to return to England, he had chosen to cast his lot in the wilderness. His reward had been swift and brutal.

Late in the day an Indian runner appeared with a letter from Thomas Spencer, the half-breed blacksmith at Oneida Castle. Gansevoort read it hastily and passed it to Willett. The tall colonel scanned it with mixed emotions. The letter read: "Just now came heere an Indian named Cannaweyyando has told a friend of his that he Left Oswego full 2 days past, that the troops are on this side Oswego & Some of them Over the falls & others in haste. they are a mind to git to Wood Creek before it is stopped. he thinks they will be heere in two Days; they are to Cross the Oneida Lake in the night; he Says the River is full of boats from Oswego to the falls; the Indian Lives in old onoyda & is one of Brandts party that was in oquage; he says there will be some boddy at Oswego to attend if treaty; there was some Strings of Wampum heere to Day to acquaint the Ind. the Treaty is to be at the 3 Rivers."

The time had come! Could they meet it? With provisions low and a fort half built? Damn Captain de la Marquisie! Curses on Jacob Cuyler, the quartermaster at Albany! Willett looked up from the note to find Gansevoort's eyes on a level with his. Gansevoort would never give in. Nor would Willett. They shook hands without comment.

In the midst of feverish activity on the fortifications, Mr. Hanson, commissary of the garrison, arrived on the last day of July from Fort Dayton to report that a number of batteaux loaded with provisions and ammunition for Stanwix had passed Dayton under guard of 200 men. Good old Cuyler! Willett was sorry he had cursed the quartermaster. If these supplies could be gotten in safely, Stanwix could hold out against the whole damned British army. Hadn't Major Bedlam arrived the day before with 150 of Colonel Weston's men from Fort Dayton, and with him Capt. de Witt and the 50 men Willett had left at that fort? Add the men in the batteaux convoy and Stanwix would have a garrison of over 700 men. Let the British come! Let Sir John Johnson and his Tories come! Let the yelling Indians come! Damn 'em! Stanwix would never surrender!

Events crowded one another. On August first three Oneidas arrived to inform Gansevoort that 100 Indians were at the Royal Block House near where Wood Creek entered Oneida Lake. Orders were issued to Capt. van Benscouten to take 100 men and three subalterns to march down the Mohawk to meet the batteaux. If these supplies were cut off, defense of the fort would be practically impossible.

Watchful waiting prevailed at the fort. Sentinels stood night and day, eagle-eyed. Scouts ranged the woods for signs of approaching Indians. About five o'clock on August 2 a cheer went up. The batteaux and their convoy had reached the Upper Landing Place. Thank God!

The whole personnel was enlisted in carrying the provisions and ammunition into the fort. Wagons of every description were pressed into service. Troopers carried tremendous loads on their backs. A steady stream moved toward the fort, slowly, persistently, being passed by a swifter current of soldiers running back to the river for more loads and empty wagons skidding along the uneven road. Firing sounded from the edge of the forest. Indians could be seen darting from tree to tree. The captain of the batteaux, sticking to his post to the last moment, was captured, but the supplies were all safely within the fort. Another hour and all would have been lost.

The Stars and Stripes

Fort Stanwix was invested on Sunday, August 3, 1777. The addition of several hundred men caused bedlam within the enclosure. Men camped in every possible inch of ground. Piles of ammunition and provisions lay everywhere, there not having been time for orderly disposition of the supplies which had been brought by the batteaux. Outside the fort stood the ample barracks of which de la Marquisie had been so proud. Gansevoort did not dare to look at them and Willett, understanding his feelings, could only grind his teeth with mortification. This was no time for "I told you so."

There was also the matter of a flag. What fort had ever been invested without displaying its colors on the ramparts? The regiments at the fort had used various flags. One with thirteen red and white cross stripes and with the familiar British cross in the center had been popular, but with the Massachusetts detachment which had accompanied the batteaux had come a newspaper announcing the resolution of Congress proclaiming a national flag for the United States of America. This flag was to consist of thirteen stripes, alternately red and white. In the blue field were to be thirteen stars, representing a new constellation. Fort Stanwix must have the new flag!

Messengers were sent scurrying about, securing pieces of material from soldiers and from the women inside the fort. An ample petticoat supplied the red stripes and ammunition shirts provided the white ones. But what could be done about the blue for the field? The problem seemed insurmountable until members of Willett's regiment recalled the blue camelot cloak that had been captured in the sortie from Fort Constitution. Capt. Abraham Swartwout was proud of that coat, which he wore only on special occasions. It was a sacrifice for him to give it up, but he did so for the American cause after receiving a promise from Gansevoort that he would be repaid later. Blue camelot cloaks did not hang on every tree, nor on every flag, for that matter, and Swartwout was a shrewd Dutchman.

Shears and needles flew in clumsy fingers. Stripes of red met stripes of white; strips of blue camelot joined uncertain strips of white in the field. When all was ready the new flag was flung from the ramparts and flashed its brilliance of red, white and blue in the bright sunlight of that Sunday morning, a sight which was greeted by the garrison with tremendous cheers.

The ceremony held the attention of the enemy long enough for a party to dash out of the fort to see what had happened to the batteaux. The men found the boats intact and also located the captain. He was wounded in the head and had been stabbed in the chest. He also had been scalped. He was brought into the fort to die.

The ramparts were crowded when the British appeared on the open plain in full view of the garrison. Orders had been issued to greet the foe in silence. The soldiers were to put their time to good advantage by counting the numbers of the enemy.

Shrill fifes broke the heaviness of the August air. The drums beat a rat-tat-tat. Line after line the British marched across the clearing, deploying as they approached. Their scarlet uniforms, taken out of packs that morning, clung to their shoulders without a wrinkle. The touches of gold on their hats and sleeves sparkled in the sunlight. And over their heads waved a multitude of flags and regimental banners. Behind them marched the Hessians, gayly arrayed in green and scarlet, with green cockades in their hats, and Johnson's Greens, irregular in dress and in precision. On the flanks danced Joseph Brant's Indians, hundreds of them, now beating time with the music, now pouring forth successions of yells which drowned the fifes and drums. Their painted bodies writhed and twisted, causing a fluttering of the feathers which seemed to grow from their shaved scalps. Ever onward sounded the steps of the regulars, steady, rhythmical, the precision of trained soldiers on parade. And always shining were the shouldered rifles, exchanging flashes of sunlight with the tomahawks of the Indians. Not a gun was fired from the ramparts. No shout of defiance answered the challenges of the Indians. The regulars and Hessians passed out of sight along the road to Fort Newport. The shrilling of the fifes sounded to the east, indicating that St. Leger was to camp behind the rise, in the ravine to the northeast of the fort. Johnson and his Indian allies returned to positions near the landing places, where the Indians kept up their shouts for hours.

Promptly at three o'clock the roll of the chamade announced the appearance of a flag from the edge of the clearing. Captain Gilbert Tice was admitted to the fort, blindfolded, and escorted to Gansevoort and Willett. He brought with him a proclamation from Colonel Barry St. Leger, the officer in command of the troops investing the fort. The unnatural rebellion had been made a "foundation for the completest system of tyranny that ever God in his displeasure suffered for a time to be exercised over a froward and stubborn generation." Tortures and imprisonment were being inflicted by assemblies calling themselves friends of liberty. Religion was being profaned. Multitudes were being compelled to swear subjection to an usurpation they abhorred.

St. Leger offered encouragement "to those whose spirit and principle may induce to partake the glorious task of redeeming their countrymen from dungeons, and reestablishing the blessings of legal government." He also promised to those who resisted him that "the messengers of justice and of wrath await them in the field and devastation, famine and every concomitant horror that a reluctant but indispensable prosecution of military must occasion, will bar the way to their return."

The proclamation sounded worthy of Johnny Burgoyne at his most bombastic moment. Strangely enough the paper did not demand immediate surrender. It said nothing at all about Fort Stanwix, leading Gansevoort and Willett to believe it to be a previously prepared document, possibly from the hand of Burgoyne. They ushered Captain Tice to the main gate, took off his blindfold and sent him on his way to St. Leger.

The main British camp could not be seen from the fort, but the Indians were active near the river. On Monday they grew bolder. They slipped from bush to bush, aiming musket shots at the sentinels and at anyone else who offered a target. A sentry discovered that fatal shots all came from the thick branches of a pine at the edge of the forest. A gun was charged with grape and fired at the tree. Down toppled a stalwart Indian who lay quivering for a moment and became still.

A party of men brought in 27 stacks of hay under cover of night. They also set fire to the isolated barn of a settler who had gone back down the river before the fort was invested.

Tuesday, the 5th, saw the destruction of de la Marquisie's barracks outside the fort. An Indian reached the building late in the afternoon and set it afire. Gusts of smoke rose above the crackling timbers and enveloped the fort, causing much coughing and cursing among the garrison. The Indians circled the fort and set up a whooping and yelling which lasted well into the night. Cannon discharged from the fort caused them to scatter, but distance brought a hideous foreboding to the shrieks which rose at intervals from the camp near the river.

Morning broke hot and heavy. The silence formed a striking contrast to the bedlam of the night before. Indians could be seen in groups toward the landing and a few British regulars marched along the edge of the clearing. Their actions puzzled Willett. Here was an army investing a fort, yet their camp seemed deserted and some men appeared to be marching away. Was it a ruse to get the defenders to make a sally after them? Conjecture gave way to concern. Gansevoort called Lieut. Diefendorf to him. Diefendorf knew the Valley well. He might get through to Schuyler, tell the general what was transpiring, and possibly bring some information. He was ordered to prepare himself for departure. This was at noon.

A shout rose from the ramparts. Willett hurried to meet three men who were running across the clearing toward the fort. The leader, a thin, swarthy, dark-haired fellow, outraced his companions to the sally port. Panting slightly, he handed the colonel a dirty paper which he had produced from beneath his hunting shirt. Willett scanned it hastily, puzzling over spelling which was worse than his own. The explanation of the enemy troop movements was now clear as the nose on his face. General Nicholas Herkimer and his Tryon County militia, marching to the relief of the fort, had camped above old Fort Schuyler the night before. Herkimer had written his message at five o'clock. The messengers should have been in long ago, but they had run afoul of Indians and had been forced to take a circuitous route. Herkimer wanted a party from the fort to meet him. The commandant at the fort was to fire three cannon to indicate that the party was leaving the fort.

Something had gone wrong. That was certain. If Herkimer had been only ten miles away the night before, he should be at the fort by now. The British had gotten wind of the militia's advance and had intercepted him. That was the reason for so much morning activity among the enemy. And here were 700 of the best troops in the Mohawk Valley standing on the ramparts waiting to be attacked, while the invaders were raising hell with the relief force. No sound of firing had been heard at the fort. Nothing had been suspected until this young runner, Adam Helmer, had arrived with Herkimer's note.

Something had to be done and done damned quickly. Gansevoort ordered a party of 200 men to be assembled and Willett volunteered to lead them. Three cannon were fired at sufficient intervals to carry the signal to Herkimer that a sally from the fort was under way.

Here Nature took a hand in the proceedings. A tremendous clap of thunder was followed by torrents of rain. Willett chafed at the bit, but there was nothing to do but wait, for damp powder was useless and the men had no bayonets. The rain ceased after an hour. The detachment marched out of the main gate toward the camp of Sir John Johnson near the river. One half the troops were from Gansevoort's regiment, the others from the Massachusetts levies.

They found Johnson's camp deserted. All was much clearer to Willett now. Johnson and his Indians had marched that morning. Only a scattering of soldiers and savages could be seen running toward the river, lugging with them such valuables as they could carry. An officer minus a coat disappeared into the woods. A soldier told Willett it was Sir John himself. The Americans opened fire. Six of the enemy were seen to drop to the ground, two of them Indians. Some soldiers rushed to scalp them, but Willett pulled them away, yelling that Americans should teach savages humanity, and not stoop to barbarism. He had not forgotten those first scalps he had seen at Ticonderoga nearly twenty years before.

The booty was spread out all around them; blankets, for which there was great need in the garrison, to the number of a hundred, also muskets, tomahawks, spears, ammunition, clothing, deerskins, kettles and Indian trinkets. The relief of Herkimer was forgotten in the frenzy for robbing the camps of their possessions. Loads of supplies were piled on the shoulders of soldiers, who staggered away toward the fort. In long lines they wound their way across the half mile of open ground between the river and the glacis. Men rushed out of the fort to aid them with their burdens. Meanwhile all stores that could not be transported were burned or otherwise destroyed.

A scout appeared, saying that St. Leger and 200 men were in the thicket on the other side of the river, about fifty yards from the line of soldiers who were coursing to the fort with the booty. Willett jumped into action. A field piece poured a salute of grapeshot into the enemy. Lines of musketry, hastily formed, fired volleys toward the advancing British. The fort entered into the fun, booming forth from the ramparts with cannon balls which brought consternation to St. Leger's force, which scampered off, leaving several red-coats lying in the mud. The procession to the fort went on without interference.

The booty was almost beyond belief. In addition to the many articles of war, there were a scarlet cloak trimmed with gold lace, three laced hats, a good deal of money in specie and paper, fifty brass kettles much needed by the garrison, a variety of clothes, also four scalps, two of them the scalps of the unfortunate berry-pickers. A bundle of unopened letters was also found, including one for Willett. Evidently the mail messenger had been killed or captured.

The five flags which had been captured were strung up on

the flagstaff beneath the American banner, while the garrison rent the air with huzzahs. A rapid check showed that Willett's detachment had not lost a single man killed or wounded. Joy reigned supreme at Fort Stanwix.

As dusk settled over the fort the sentinels could see soldiers straggling along the edge of the clearing. Their green uniforms were soiled and bloody. Some dragged themselves along painfully; others were being carried by companions. Surely something dreadful had taken place, something of which the fort was totally ignorant. From the Indian camp rose the cries of returning warriors, naked except for their gay paint and breechclouts, bewailing the loss of their blankets and kettles.

A figure emerged from the gloom and approached the fort. A sentry challenged him, received a favorable reply and admitted him to the fort. From his lips Willett and Gansevoort learned of the tragedy at Oriskany. General Herkimer had sent out Helmer and the other two messengers. He had waited for the signal from the fort. Colonel Ebenezer Cox had become impatient. He had called Herkimer a coward and a Tory. Right to his face. In desperation the gallant general had ordered an advance. The militia had been ambushed in a ravine at Oriskany. Colonel Visscher's rear guard had fled. Bloody fighting had taken place, hand to hand fighting with tomahawks, knives and fists. General Herkimer had been wounded in the leg and knocked from his horse. He had sat under a tree, drawn up his men in a square, directed the fighting, all the while smoking his pipe to keep his mind off the pain in his leg. A shower had stopped hostilities for an hour, just as the shots from the fort had been heard. The militia had repelled an attack from Johnson's Greens, after which both sides, broken and disorganized, had fled in disorder, leaving their dead and wounded on the field. Herkimer had been put in a batteau and taken to his home. Cox was dead. Dr. Younglove was dead. Thomas Spencer was dead. Many other brave men had fallen. Some had been captured. All had been lost.

Colonel Marinus Willett wrote in his Orderly Book that night for the first time since August first. There wasn't much to write. Actions spoke louder than words. But, with a firm hand, he entered: "Parole—Unity. Countersign—Success."

The Dangerous Mission

THE DAY AFTER ORISKANY DAWNED QUIETLY. The garrison, still gloating over the successful sortie, was anticipating distribution of plunder which littered the enclosure. The British had little time for insults or musketry and the Indians, robbed of their possessions, sulked in their camp. The British spent the morning constructing three batteries which they brought into action without effect. After darkness fell they approached the glacis in groups, called to the Americans and challenged them to come out and fight with fixed bayonets. Shouts of scorn and laughter caused them to beat a hasty retreat to their camp. At midnight Adam Helmer, accompanied by his two companions and the militiaman who had come in with the ghastly news of Oriskany, slid out of the sally port and melted into the darkness. They carried with them orders from Gansevoort to notify Colonel Weston at Fort Dayton of the situation within Stanwix.

Friday was ushered in by a salvo of shells from the British batteries. The garrison returned it with solid shot. Late in the afternoon a flag approached from the British camp, accompanied by three officers, two clad in scarlet, the third in the green of Butler's Rangers. They advanced boldly under the steady beating of the chamade and were challenged by the sentry. They requested to present a message to the commanding officer. They were blindfolded and conducted into Gansevoort's dining room, where they blinked as the cloths were removed from their eyes. The windows had been shut, thus prohibiting any view of the outer court. Candles twinkled from a table upon which cheese, crackers and wine had been placed. At the further end sat Colonels Gansevoort, Willett and Mellen, clad in coarse green and gray regimentals, their set jaws jutting from stocks of soiled white. Behind them ranged the lesser officers of the fort, crowded into every available inch of space, their faces cold and unfriendly. At a gesture from Gansevoort the British seated themselves across the boards from the three frowning colonels. Wine was passed and a lame attempt made at conversation. It was obviously no time for exchange of pleasantries.

Major Ancrom, adjutant to Colonel St. Leger, wasted no time in coming to the point. He was an important fellow, stiff and grave in his bright regimentals, crisp and abrupt in his speech. "Gentlemen," he announced, "I am directed by Colonel St. Leger, the officer who commands the army now investing the garrison, to inform the commandant that the colonel has, with much difficulty, prevailed on the Indians to agree, that if the garrison, without further resistance, shall be delivered up, with the public stores belonging to it, to the investing army, the officers and soldiers shall have all their baggage and private property secured to them. And in order that the garrison may have a special pledge to this effect, Colonel Butler accompanies me to assure them, that not a hair of the head of any one of them shall be hurt."

Major Ancrom paused, took a sip of his wine and turned to the officer in green who sat at his side. "That, I think, was the expression they made use of, was it not?"

Colonel John Butler nodded.

Major Ancrom continued his discourse: "I am likewise directed to remind the commandant, that the defeat of General Herkimer must deprive the garrison of all hopes of relief, especially as General Burgoyne is now at Albany; so that, sooner or later, the fort must fall into our hands. Colonel St.

Leger, from an earnest desire to prevent further bloodshed, hopes these terms will not be refused; as in this case it will be out of his power to make them again. It was with great difficulty that the Indians consented to the present arrangement, as it will deprive them of that plunder which they always calculate upon on similar occasions. Should, then, the present terms be rejected, it will be out of the power of the colonel to restrain the Indians, who are very numerous and much exasperated, not only from plundering the property, but destroying the lives of probably the greater part of the garrison. Indeed the Indians are so exceedingly provoked and mortified by the losses they have sustained in the late actions, having had several of their favorite chiefs killed, that they threaten—" Ancrom paused and glanced around the room—"and the colonel, if the present arrangements should not be entered into, will not be able to prevent them from executing the threats to march down the country and destroy the settlement with its inhabitants. In this case, not only men, but women and children, will experience the sad effects of their vengeance. These considerations, it is ardently hoped, will procure a proper effect and induce the commandant, by complying with the terms now offered, to save himself from future regret when it will be too late."

Silence greeted this display of bombast. Major Ancrom, surprised and chagrined, stared haughtily at the stony faces across the table. Behind them the flickering light of the candles threw into indistinct relief the set jaws and folded arms of the officers of the garrison. Colonel Butler, who must have had a premonition of the result, stared sulkily at the table. He knew better than the Britisher the disregard of frontier officers for threats and empty promises. After years of dealing with Indians, he could not trust them beyond the reach of his voice. One white man, and one only, had held the trust and confidence of the Iroquois. Colonel Butler had been that man's most intimate friend, but Sir William Johnson had been dead these three years.

Gansevoort's pleasant face turned more florid than ever. His gray eyes were mere slits. On either side sat Willett and Mellen, their leathery cheeks drawn toward their chins, their brows knit over prominent noses. In the tense silence the voices of soldiers at play in the court drifted through the wooden shutters, carefree voices of American youth enjoying themselves even though their lives hung in the balance. Gansevoort signalled for Willett to reply to the British demands. The New Yorker was better suited to the task than was the shy Dutchman.

Marinus Willett rose to his feet, his angular frame erect, his hair brushing the ceiling. He did not use pretty words. Staring Ancrom full in the face he asked, "Do I understand you, Sir? I think you say that you come from a British colonel who is the commander of the army that invests this fort; and by your uniform you appear to be an officer in the British service. You have made a long speech on the occasion of your visit which, stripped of all its superfluities, amounts to this: that you come from a British colonel to the commandant of this garrison to tell him that if he does not deliver up the garrison into the hands of your colonel he will send his Indians to murder our women and children. You will be pleased to reflect, Sir, that their blood will be on your head, not on ours. We are doing our duty; this garrison is committed to our charge and we will take care of it. After you get out of it, you may turn around and look at its outside, but never expect to come in again, unless you come as prisoners. I consider the message you have brought a degrading one for a British officer to send and by no means reputable for a British officer to carry. For my own part, I declare, before I would consent to deliver this garrison to such a murdering set as your army, by your own account, consists of, I would suffer my body to be filled with splinters and set on fire, as you know has at times been practiced by such hordes of women and children killers as belong to your army."

No silence after this refusal to surrender. Cheers broke from the throats of the assembled officers. Louder echoes rose from the enclosure outside. Gansevoort and Mellen smiled. Willett, his whole body ablaze with wrath and indignation, still stood shaking a long finger at Major Ancrom. And that officer understood, as Colonel Butler had known, that Stanwix was a fort that would never surrender. Isolated, beset on all sides, with provisions and ammunition diminishing, there was something within the fort that was now clear to the dapper British officer; it was the spirit of young America, the unconquerable determination to survive which lay deep within breasts hidden by coarse waistcoats of Russian drilling. Boasts and threats would not crush that spirit. Major Ancrom knew he was beaten, so he closed the interview by asking permission for his surgeon to examine wounded Britishers held by the garrison. He also requested a cessation of hostilities for three days. These concessions were granted by Gansevoort. Butler, Ancrom and the other officer, who had sat erect in his scarlet and gold, were blindfolded and led into the court, where they stood, silent and defeated, listening to the huzzahs of the garrison. A half hour later their flag moved away from the fort, the drummer beating out the step with a courage he did not feel.

Gansevoort wasted no time. Much could be accomplished in three days. He had not been fully satisfied with Adam Helmer as a messenger. It had taken that scout too long to reach the fort on the fatal day of Oriskany. He might dally with the news to Dayton. Gansevoort voiced his apprehensions to Willett, who volunteered to run the British lines and go down the Valley for relief. Willett asked for Levi Stockwell as a companion, for the lieutenant was known as a good hunter who was familiar with the Indian method of travelling in the wilderness. Willett, despite his willingness and his years of experience in frontier fighting, was a city man with scant knowledge of the forest.

An hour after midnight on August 9th the two officers left the sally port, stepped cautiously along the edge of the marsh and angled toward the Mohawk River. In order that they might travel unencumbered, they carried no muskets or baggage. Their sole weapons were eight-foot spears known as espontons, which also denoted military rank. They had tucked a few crackers and bits of cheese into the pockets of their hunting shirts and Willett had slipped a quart canteen of spirits against his chest.

Stockwell discovered a log which had been thrown across the river, which was narrow and shallow at this point. Inch by inch they slid along the log on their bellies, their feet dragging in the water. The tramp of a sentry could be heard as he paced up and down the shore. Once they were across the stream, the two messengers felt their way through the darkness, their espontons probing the ground before them, their eyes straining to detect shapes of trees and fallen logs. The Indian camp was near, for the Iroquois, after Willett's sortie had stripped them of their belongings, had moved across the river.

Sharply against the silence rose the bark of a dog. Stockwell grasped Willett's arm and pushed his companion toward the trunk of a large tree and pressed his own body against the bark. In a whisper he informed his superior officer that it would be unwise to go further until there was more light. The two men stood silently, braced against the tree, for what seemed to Willett an eternity and which was in reality several hours. Borne on the breeze, the sentry-calls from Stanwix told them that all was well at the fort. The Indian camp lay asleep. The dog, satisfied that no one was about, or discouraged by lack of response to his effort, had quieted down.

The two officers started with the morning star. Stockwell,

in the lead, altered his direction. Instead of proceeding in a straight line toward the German Flatts settlement, he took a northerly course which carried them through tangled undergrowth toward the winding Mohawk. He and his companion waded in and out of the river several times. When they reached a spot where they could step on stones and thus leave no trail, they forsook the Mohawk and tramped north for several hours before continuing their course east. They travelled all day, stopping occasionally for breath or for a drink from a spring. Night caught them. They halted in a wood and refreshed themselves with crackers and cheese and a few nips from Willett's canteen. They dared not chance a fire, for Indians were lurking all along the Valley. They lay down, wrapped in each other's arms, to keep off the cold of a northern night.

Stiff and chilled, they finished their crackers at dawn and continued their journey. Willett limped badly, for he had contracted rheumatism in one knee. The two men, walking slowly and cautiously, began to shift their course to the south and the river. About nine o'clock the woods suddenly opened. Before them spread an endless swath of fallen timber, stretching as far as the eye could reach. Stockwell told Willett that they had struck the "hurricane," a lane which, according to the Indians, had been gouged out of the forest by a storm some years before, leaving the timber broken and strewn on the ground. Berry bushes had sprung up in profusion. Raspberries, dead ripe, hung in clusters from the young bushes. Willett and his companion, their throats parched and their stomachs empty, pounced on the berries with childish glee and satisfied their thirst and hunger with huge handfuls of the red thimbles.

They followed the "hurricane" for several miles, keeping to the high lands above the river. The day turned hot and sultry. Perspiration poured from them, but they tramped on, hoping to reach Fort Dayton before nightfall. Though Willett's knee had limbered up, he had no desire to spend another night in the woods. Furthermore, time constituted the chief element in their success. The first straggling clearings appeared below them early in the afternoon and the charred remains of homesteads burned by Indian raids were black against the green fields. They staggered into Fort Dayton at three o'clock and were welcomed heartily by Colonel Weston, from whom they learned that Adam Helmer and his companions had arrived on the ninth bearing an account of affairs at Fort Stanwix. Chairman Peter Dygert of the German Flatts Committee had sent Helmer on to Albany with the story of Oriskany and an appeal for assistance. Weston had learned that General Learned had left Van Schaick's Island with his brigade of Massachusetts troops. They should be somewhere in the Valley. Having heard this news, Willett and Stockwell begged only one boon—sleep.

Walter Butler Is Tried

THE TWO OFFICERS RODE DOWN THE VALLEY the next morning on horses provided by Colonel Weston. Toward dusk they met the Massachusetts brigade and learned that the relief troops were to be commanded by General Benedict Arnold, who was in Albany recruiting more men.

They found the Connecticut general in a calm, determined mood. Arnold had gone into a fit of passion when news had come that Congress had passed unfavorably on his question of rank. He had resigned immediately. Schuyler, harassed on every side and waiting for General Horatio Gates to supersede him, had pleaded with Arnold to remain in the army, for Schuyler was reluctant to allow such a capable officer to sulk in his tent at a time when the United States faced a crisis. Dygert's letter had arrived, telling of Herkimer's desperate wound, of the death of Ebenezer Cox and the disaster which had befallen the flower of the Tryon County militia at Oriskany. Schuyler had called a council of brigadiers, had implored them to send relief and had won them over. Arnold, seeing a chance for personal glory, had volunteered to command the relief party. Once appointed he had been indefatigable in recruiting and dispatching troops.

Arnold was ready to advance, so Willett and Stockwell rode with him up the Mohawk Valley. They reached Schenectady on the 15th and a day or two later they approached the German Flatts. Willett, deeply concerned over the fate of the hero of Oriskany, asked permission of Arnold to stop at Herkimer's house on the south bank of the river below Fort Herkimer. Willett visited the militia leader on August 19th, almost two weeks after the battle of Oriskany. They chatted while Dr. Johnson, who had amputated Herkimer's leg that day, cleaned out the festering wound. Herkimer was sitting up in bed when Willett left that evening; an active pipe projected from the general's lips and he seemed to be in the best of spirits.

The following morning, at an inn six miles to the west, Willett learned that Herkimer had died in the night. The general had joked with his servants, had called for his Bible and had bled to death, silently. That his death was due to improper treatment, Willett had no doubt. Either the amputation should not have been performed or, if performed, it should have been done above the knee, for the doctor had discovered after the amputation that the fracture of the bone extended higher up than where the limb had been removed, thus preventing him from securing the arteries properly.

A discouraged and disgruntled Willett rode into Fort Dayton on that 20th of August, 1777. He found Arnold in a fighting mood. The preceding evening, while Herkimer lay dying in his hip-roofed brick mansion beside the river, Colonel Weston had received information that Walter Butler, son of Colonel John Butler, was across the Mohawk at the house of the Tory Shoemaker, whom he had induced to gather together the Loyalists in the area. Weston had sent a detachment to surround the rambling Shoemaker residence. Butler, trapped, had surrendered along with Hon Yost Schuyler and other Tories. Butler now sulked in the Fort Dayton guardhouse. Arnold showed Willett the proclamation which had been taken from Butler.

"Camp before Fort Stanwix, August 13, 1777.
"To the Inhabitants of Tryon County:

"Notwithstanding the many and great injuries we have received in person and property at your hands, and being at the head of victorious troops, we most ardently wish to have peace restored to this once happy country; to obtain which, we are willing and desirous, upon a proper submission on your parts, to bury into oblivion all that is past, and hope that you are, or will be, convinced in the end that we were your friends and good advisers, and not such wicked, designing men, as those who led you into error, and almost total ruin. You have, no doubt, great reason to dread the resentment of the Indians, on account of the loss they sustained in the late action, and the mulish obstinacy of your troops in the garrison, who have no resource but in themselves; for which reasons the Indians declare, that if they do not surrender the garrison without further opposition, they will put every soul to death, not only the garrison, but the whole country, without any regard to age, sex, or friends; for which reason it has become your indispensable duty, as you must answer the consequences, to send a deputation of your principal people to oblige them immediately to what, in a very little time must be enforced, the surrender of the garrison; in which case we will engage, on the faith of Christians, to protect you from the violence of the Indians.

"Surrounded as you are by victorious armies, one half (if not the greater part) of the inhabitants friends to the government, without any resource, surely you can not hesitate a moment to accept the terms proposed to you by friends and well wishers to the country."

This proclamation was signed by John Johnson, D. W. Claus and John Butler, Superintendents.

Heretofore, the British had been dealing with Herkimer, Gansevoort and Willett, brave and excellent soldiers, but men unaccustomed to the exchange of bombast characteristic of generals of the period. In Arnold they met their equal. The Connecticut general immediately ordered a court martial to try Butler and asked Willett to sit as Judge Advocate. In response to Butler's proclamation, the general penned one of his own:

"By the Honorable Benedict Arnold, Esquire, major general and commander-in-chief of the army of the United States of America, on the Mohawk River:

"Whereas a certain Barry St. Leger, a British general in the service of the —— George of Great Britain, at the head of a banditti of Robbers, murderers and traitors, composed of savages of America and more savage Britons, among whom is a noted Sir John Johnson, John Butler and Daniel Claus, have lately appeared on the frontiers of this state, and have threatened ruin and destruction to all the inhabitants of the United States, they have also, by artifice and misrepresentation, induced many of the ignorant and unwary subjects of these states to forfeit their allegiance to the same, and join them in their atrocious crimes and parties of treachery and parricide. Humanity to these poor deluded wretches, who are hastening blindfold to destruction, induces me to offer them and all others concerned, whether savages, Germans, Americans or Britons, pardon, provided they do within ten days from the date hereof come and lay down their arms, sue for protection and swear allegiance to the United States of America. But if still blind to their own safety, they obstinately persist in their wicked courses, determined to draw on themselves the just vengeance of heaven, and of this exasperated country, they must expect no mercy from either."

Walter Butler was tried that day. Colonel Willett, as Judge Advocate, wrote down the details of the trial:

"Proceedings of Generall Court Martial held at the house

of Mr. Peter Doxtator at the German Flats, August 20th, 1777, by order of the Honorable Major General Arnold, for the tryal of such prisoners as shall be brought before him.

Colonel Bayley, *President*
members

Lieut Colo Brooks	Captn Allen
Major Hall	Lieut Haywood
Captain McCracken	Lieut Whelp
Captn Hicks	Lieut Cone
Captn Keeth	Lieut Van Valkenburgh
Captn Livingston	Lieut Eldridge

Lieut Colonel Willett Judge Advocate

"The Members being met and duly sworn, the Judge Advocate being also sworn, and prosecuting in behalf of the American States—

"Walter Butler an Ensign in the Kings or 8th regiment, in the service of the King of England with whom these states are at war, was brought Prisoner before the Court, and charged with being a Traytor and Spy, in that under the pretence of being a Flagg from the Enemy he was found endeavouring to sudduce a number of the inhabitance of this state from there aligiance to the United States of America.

"To which charge the prisoner upon being Challenged pleads. Not guilty.

"The Court then proceded to the examination of a Number of evidences in support of the said Charge.

"William Petre (evidence) being Sworn saith that he heard a few days ago that the Prisoner was at one Mr. Shoemakers (who lives about two miles from this house) as a flagg. That he enquired whether the prisoner had sent to any of the Committee but did not understood he had. That Capt. Tygert Chairman of the Committee sent for him to go to see the Prisoner. That he went to Mr. Shoemakers and there found Captain Tygert, who had a parcell of papers which he got from the prisoner, among which was a Proclamation from Barry St. Ledger Commander of a Detachment of the Enemies forces, with a letter from Colonels Claus & Butler & Sir John Johnson likewise in the enemies service and another letter sign by Jn Fry & Fred. Bellinger two Prisoners with the enemy, all directed to the inhabitance of Tryon County. That the prisoner desired an answer to these papers as soon as possible directing himself to Captain Tygert. That Captain Tygert, Questioned the Prisoner about a man of his party going about to sedduce the inhabitance from there Aligiance but the Prisoner denyed knowing anything about it—The Prisoner asked the evidence whether he did not ask them if they where the Proper persons to apply to? Ans: Not that he knows. Whether he did not say he would keep his people together and remain at Mr. Shoemakers? Ans: Yes. Whether they did not desire the Prisoner should wait for an answer or untill he should hear from them? Ans: No. Judge Advo: What did you understand to be the sence of those papers? Ans: for the inhabitance to Lay down there arms and receive protection from the British troops. Court: What was the purpose of the Prisoners Conversation with the people? he does not know it was between the prisoner and Capt. Tygert. Pri: Whether he did not hear Capt. Tygert say that he came from Genll Harkaman? An: No.

"Mr. Shoemaker being sworn, saith that the prisoner came to his house and said he was a flagg, and that he had a proclamation from Generl St. Ledger to the inhabitance, and got him to send a letter to the inhabitance to meet him at some place, and that a number of the inhabitance came to his house to meet the prisoner. That there conversation was concering the said Proclamation. Presid: What time did he come to your house? Ans: About 9 O'clock in the Morning, and a Number of armed men with him. Membr: Did you hear anything said about making applycation to the officer commanding the troops here? An: No. Pris: Whether he did not hear him enquire who was the proper person to answer those papers? An: Yes, but knows not what answer he got.

"Capt. Whiley being sworn, saith, that the day the prisoner came down he went to see him and enquired of his business, and why he did not enquire for the Commanding Officer if he had any business to do—that the Prisoner said he knew of no Commanding Officer nor any Majestrate or other person in Authority, except Mr. Shoemaker who was a Justice of peace, and that his business was with the inhabitance. The Prisoner asked him whether he did not tell him he was ignorant of there laws & knew of none but the inhabitance had pointed out the Committee & Genll Harkaman and that if the Committee sent him to any other person he was willing to go to them. Ans: No, but that he desspised all there constitution and endeavoured to perswade the inhabitance to lay down there arms, by a Number of Arguments he used to work upon there fears for that purpose.

"Doctor Thomas being sworn saith, that on hearing their was a flagg at Mr. Shoemakers, he went to see who it was & found the prisoner among the number of the inhabitance, arguing with them and endeavouring to perswade them to lay down there arms, and that there was a number of Indians and armed men with the prisoner. The Prisoner asked him if he did not apply to the inhabitance, who was to answer him in his business. An: No, but that upon his recommending the prisoner to apply to Col. Weston the Officer Commanding at Fort Dayton he answered him that his business was with the inhabitance, that he knew no Colonel Weston nor Fort Dayton.

"Lieu. Welsh being sworn saith, that he likewise went to see the said flagg, and enquired about his business, and why he did not enquire for the commanding officer? That the Prisoner said he had nothing to do with any commanding officer. That his business was with the inhabitance and addressing himself to them he assured them that if they did not lay down there arms the most horrid Carnage must ensue from the enraged Savages.

"Colonel Brooks examined at the desire of the prisoner being sworn saith that he was ordered by Col Weston to go out with a Detachment who was to enquire about the business of the said flagg. That he went & saw the prisoner who told him he had seen the Committee who had promised to answer him. That he returned to Col Weston who upon an interview with the Committee was told by them that they did not view him as a flagg but a seducecer of the inhabitance and that not without a considerable deal of difficulty he afterwards took him & his party. The Prisoner then asked him if he did not say that if the Committee sent him to Col Weston he was willing to go there? An: Not that he remember.

"The Evidence being finished & the Prisoner & spectators withdrawn, the Court proceed to form judgment.

"The Court upon due consideration of the whole matter before them, is of opinion that Walter Butler the said prisoner is Guilty of being a spy—and adjudge him to suffer the pain and penalty of Death—

"Joseph Schuyler charged with deserting from the armey of the American States and going over to the Enemy, was brought Prisoner before the Court, who upon being Challenged pleads Guilty.

"The Court adjudge that the said Joseph Schuyler receive 100 lashes upon his bare back & that he be confined dureing the Generals pleasure—

"And then the Court adjourned untill further orders.

"The aforesaid proceedings being signed by the President was Carried to the General for his acceptance.

"State of New York German Flats August 20th 1777—

M. Willett Judge Advocate"

Marinus Willett carried his report of proceedings to General Arnold, who approved it and ordered that Butler be hanged the following day. Willett communicated this news to the prisoner, who received it without comment.

The execution was not carried out. Walter Butler had friends in Arnold's forces. A group of officers, influential citizens of Albany, petitioned the general for a respite. Arnold granted it reluctantly and Butler was sent to Albany. His escape a year later brought devastation and ruin to Cherry Valley.

"The Devil"

ARNOLD ASKED WILLETT if the garrison at Fort Stanwix was in any immediate danger, for he was reluctant to march to its relief with what he believed to be an inferior force. He also told Willett that Gates had superseded Schuyler in command of the Northern Department at Van Schaick's Island, where he was receiving continual reinforcements. Was Willett willing to take another trip to Albany and ask Gates for the Second and Fourth New York regiments? The colonel was willing to go, but was it necessary to have more troops for the relief party? Stanwix was holding out pretty well. It would never surrender, relief party or no relief party.

Nevertheless Willett and Stockwell rode down the Valley once more, this time to see General Gates, who received them, invited them to dinner, and promised the requested regiments, a promise which was never fulfilled. In his relations with Gates and Arnold, the tall colonel must have learned much about generals to disgust him.

Willett and Stockwell rode back to Fort Dayton, where they learned that Arnold had summoned confidence to go to the relief of Fort Stanwix. He had used a clever ruse to drive off the British. Hon Yost Schuyler, who had been captured with Butler, was a mentally incompetent offspring of a prominent family. He had consented to go to St. Leger with the news that the American forces were greater in number than the leaves on the trees. When Arnold reached the fort St.

Leger was miles away on his retreat to Canada. Hon Yost's news may have sent the colonel packing, but it is more probable that accurate information from Molly Brant or some Tory caused his retreat.

Willett and Stockwell rode back to the fort which held for them so much of pride and success. They forded the Mohawk near old Fort Schuyler and rode up the south bank. A sudden impurity struck their nostrils, an odor which increased in intensity after they had forded Oriskany Creek. Near a small stream a gun stood against a tree with a pair of boots hanging to it; in the water lay the owner, black, putrid. A little distance away lay a well-dressed man without hat or coat; a black handkerchief circled his head. His limbs were so swollen that his deerskin breeches were rent from top to bottom, exposing putrid flesh. A little further on an Indian was seen hanging to the limb of a tree, suspended by a harness. Nearby the body of an American militiaman was pinned to a tree several feet from the ground by a bayonet driven through his abdomen. Such had been Oriskany.

After making a wide detour the two messengers entered Fort Stanwix. Major Cochran told Willett with a smile that General Arnold had excused Gansevoort so that he could visit his "dear Caty."

Willett took command with his usual efficiency. A letter went forward to General Gates revealing the scarcity of ammunition at the fort, only a few shells and no fuses being available for the captured cohorns. The supply of salt pork would last but eight days. The men were at work on the fortifications. They could not labor on empty stomachs. With the lifting of the siege, there was a corresponding relaxation among the soldiers, a carelessness in speech and manners which brought the following rebuke from Willett: "The Commandant is very sorry to hear the idle as well as Sinfull Custom of profane Cursing and Swearing practiced in the Garrison A practice that while it can afford no kind of

Pleasure or profit to the person who uses it; is a Transgression of the Laws of our Country as well as of our God, and can be productive of no other Consequence than those of procuring the Discipline of Heaven, and Offending the Thoughtfull Virtuous Ear. It is therefore Strongly Recommended to the Officers and Soldiers of this Garrison to refrain from so unnecessary a practice." Profiteers were also troublesome. On September 23 the colonel wrote in his Orderly Book: "Such persons as have cows at this garrison are to remember that they receive their feed from the publick. Six pence per quart is the highest price that they may receive for milk. If any Person is found to make more than that price, their cows will be delivered over for the use of the sick in the hospital." On the 28th a party was sent to Oriskany to collect and draw all hay which lay in the fields and have it properly stacked for use of the garrison.

Gansevoort returned that day from his visit to "dear Caty" and addressed the garrison, complimenting them on their excellent work during the siege and relaying to them the fine things he had heard about them while he was in Albany. He also brought news of the successes of other American armies.

Willett left Fort Stanwix, visited the army near Saratoga and went on to Fishkill to see Mrs. Willett. He also visited the Grand Army at White Marsh, twelve miles from Philadelphia. When he returned to Fort Stanwix on February 23, 1778, Gansevoort handed him a letter. Congress, grateful to Colonel Marinus Willett for his work during the sortie at Fort Stanwix, had awarded him an "elegant sword." Unfortunately, Congress had neglected to send the sword with the resolution.

Discipline at the fort had relaxed during Willett's absence. Gansevoort, who had married "dear Caty" in January, was probably thinking more of his wife than he was about martial affairs. An outbreak of smallpox plus a spell of cold weather had cast fear into the hearts of the garrison. Willett, unable to witness the sufferings of the soldiers, ordered that they be allowed to keep fires at night and dispatched a sergeant and two privates to make the rounds of the barracks every hour from tattoo to reveille to prevent damage by fire. As warmer weather approached he set men to work draining the swamp contiguous to the fort. Clothes were to be kept clean and whole as possible. Beds were to be turned up daily and bedding aired. The apartments were to be swept every day and scrubbed on Saturdays.

Inactivity bored the troops. Willett himself, after his visit to the Grand Army, was discontented with duty at Stanwix. He, together with several other officers, signed a petition to be transferred to a field of greater activity and usefulness, declaring their wish to learn the art of war. Gansevoort received the request calmly, as was his custom, but wrote a formal reply, disapproving of their request and pointing out to them the importance of Stanwix as a frontier outpost.

Hogs were straying near the fort and injuring the works. Willett ordered them ringed. Carpenters were selling rum to the soldiers without permission. They received a word of caution from Willett, but one carpenter, transgressing the law, sold rum and received a soldier's blanket in exchange. No more rum was allotted to him. The milk profiteers were also cornered. A farmer who was caught selling milk for nine pence a quart had his cows confiscated for use in the hospital.

Army reforms in April caused several of the officers at the fort to be dropped from the rolls. Among them were Levi Stockwell, the companion on Willett's trip to Fort Dayton, and Abraham Swartwout, whose camelot cloak had become part of the first American flag to be flown by a fort under investiture by the enemy.

The Oneida and Tuscarora Indians, who had been faithful to the American cause, were being ostracised by the other Iroquois nations. Their distress and poverty were pleaded in a letter from Oneida Castle. Willett not only replied to the letter, and sent the Oneidas a small supply of powder and lead, but he visited their castle on April 10.

The Marquis de Lafayette came to Fort Johnstown that spring to meet the Oneidas in hope of gaining their support for an expedition to Canada. The Indians exacted a promise from him that the United States would send a man to help them to improve their fortifications. The engineer, de Tousard, evidently took a liking to Willett, who helped him to gather a party of 47 Indians to visit Lafayette at Valley Forge. De Tousard wrote Willett at length, thanking him for his assistance, also informing him of troubles on the road when the Indians had lagged behind to drink rum. Lafayette also wrote, saying that the Indians had set up such a noise as to frighten both the horses and the British.

News of the French Alliance reached Fort Stanwix on May 12th. Messrs. James Dean and Samuel Kirkland were leaving for the council of the Confederate Nations of Indians assembled at Onondaga. Willett knew that authority for a proclamation lay in the hands of General Schuyler, then head of Indian affairs, but time pressed and the news of the alliance might have a profound effect on the Indians, so he addressed the Oneidas and Tuscaroras, commending them on their loyalty and asking for it to continue. His proclamation was penned in the most flattering language he could assume, for he was a firm believer in conciliating Indians with compliments and appeals to their vanity. The most flowery paragraph read:

"Brothers—I make no doubt but You will Rejoice with us on this occasion. The Accounts I give you are no deception they are true. And you know very well that we have always given you truer Accounts. We have to boast that we have not done like our Enemies and Especially that vile of all Lyers Butler, who has been Continually spreading false Reports among You to deceive and Destroy you. Our Cause being good and just it never stood in need of any false reports to support it. God has witnessed to the justness of it, in affording us his Assistance, and We have had the pleasure of triumphing gloriously over our Enemies. We now behold our Country rising from its Difficulties, and our Enemies humbling themselves at our Feet."

Willett saw Dean and Kirkland off before writing to Schuyler and explaining his action.

A general celebration was held at the fort on May 30 in honor of the French Alliance. To climax it a *feu-de-joie* was fired from the ramparts at one o'clock.

Gansevoort, who had been visiting "dear Caty," returned a few days later. Marinus Willett bade Fort Stanwix farewell. He left with the garrison a long poem entitled, "Genl Harkemer's Battle, A New Song to the Tune of the British Boys." It was dedicated "To the Field Officers of the 3d New York Battalion by their very humble servant, Juvenus, Albany Dec. 5, 1777." The closing stanzas follow:

"But here to end my ditty
Euterpe does refuse
The New York 3d Battalion too
Are fav'rites of My Muse
Who after this important Day
Heroic firmness did display
And keep their hellish foes in play
Till help might be obtained.

Long live their Colo. Gansevoort
Of celebrated Name
And may brave Colo. Willett's deeds
Dwell on the wings of Fame
Bold Major Cochran we extol
The Captains and subalterns all
With the whole Regiment great and small
Forever shine their Name."

The Grand Army

WILLETT REACHED PEEKSKILL on the same day in June that General Gates received word of the evacuation of Philadelphia by the British. Gates sent him to General Washington with a statement of his force and magazines. Willett reached the New Jersey camp of the Grand Army that evening, gave Washington Gates' information, had a brief conversation, and received permission to remain with the Grand Army on condition that he would return later to the Mohawk Valley, where Washington thought his services most valuable.

Willett introduced himself to General Scott of Virginia, who was to harass the enemy with his detachment of light troops. Scott accepted Willett as a volunteer aide. Scott's troops were five miles north of Monmouth Court House, where the left wing of the British army under Lord Cornwallis had camped for the night. General Charles Lee, in command of 600 Continental troops, had definite orders from Washington to gain the flank of the enemy and attack it vigorously while the Commander-in-Chief came up from behind to pinch Cornwallis and Sir Henry Clinton.

June 28th broke hot and sultry. Clinton began to advance cautiously toward Sandy Hook. Knyphausen and his Hessians marched rapidly along the Middletown Road until they had gained a point more than a mile beyond Monmouth Court House. Scott, with the left wing of Lee's division, was swinging to cut off Knyphausen, who was caught in the trap.

Wayne and Lafayette were threatening Cornwallis. Lafayette galloped up with an order for Scott to attack. It was countermanded by Lee, much to the surprise and indignation of Scott. A rumor filtered through to Willett that Lee had declared that the Continentals could not stand up against British regulars.

Scott established himself in a good defensive position and waited for Lee to change his mind. Nothing happened, so Scott sent Willett to inform Lee of his advantageous position. Willett met General Anthony Wayne. They saw Lee and rode rapidly to him in time to hear him say, "The enemy have too much cavalry for us." Calling his dog, Lee rode toward the rear.

The retreating Continentals managed to halt a British cavalry attack and a charge by a regiment of Highlanders.

General Washington appeared, mounted on a large sorrel horse, within the line of the enemy's fire. Spy-glass in hand, he "seemed to observe and know everything." Willett, writing of the scene many years later, stated: "His noble countenance displayed the greatness of his mind; and his whole demeanor was calculated to command veneration. I have seen him in a variety of situations, and none in which he did not appear great; but never did I see him when he exhibited such greatness as on this day."

Willett, noting Washington's dangerous position, sent an aide to warn him. Washington wheeled his horse and retired to safer ground. Willett, returning to his own outfit, heard a man remark, "Poor Lee!" Willett asked if Lee had been shot, whereupon his informant replied, "No, but he is a great deal worse off, for the general has given him a most severe reprimand, and ordered him to English Town (four miles in the rear) with orders to collect such scattered troops as he might find and assemble them at that place."

The main body of the Continental forces came up. General Nathanael Greene planted a battery which raked the enemy lines with deadly effect. Wayne conducted a frontal attack. Baron von Steuben, with three brigades, menaced the British rear. The British, after stubborn resistance, retreated toward Sandy Hook. The Continentals, learning that the enemy had returned to New York, crossed the Hudson River at Stony Point and went into camp near White Plains.

Willett rode back ahead of the Grand Army. He had enjoyed his taste of battle, but Washington had convinced him that his chief duty lay on the frontier. He chuckled to himself at a description of the tilt between Washington and Lee. According to a sergeant Washington had ridden up to Lee and yelled, "My God! General Lee, what are you about?" When Lee had refused to answer, His Excellency had ordered him to the rear with the remark, "Damned poltroon!"

At Danbury Willett found Mary worried because she had not heard from Young Marinus. The letter, dated July 14, arrived on August 7th. It was from Dr. McKnight. There wasn't much the doctor could say. Young Marinus, worn out from his exertions, had been taken ill with fever. He had died after an illness of a few days.

Willett had much time that winter to think about his loss, for the Grand Army camped in Westchester, threatening but not daring to attack the British in New York. He went about like a man in a dream, without incentive, without hope. Mary also worried him, so he visited her as often as possible at New Windsor, to which village she had moved after the British raid on Danbury.

The Sullivan Expedition

GOVERNOR GEORGE CLINTON WAS WORRIED about the Mohawk Valley. Since the raids of the year before on Cherry Valley and Wyoming, confidence had departed from the frontier. William Harper of the Tryon County Committee had written that "there would not be one Whig living on the Mohock River above Sconackendy by the first of May." If the militia had a leader, they might protect the scattered settlements, but since the death of Nicholas Herkimer no one had been able to assume that responsibility with success. One man had the respect of the entire Mohawk Valley—Marinus Willett.

Clinton wrote to General Washington, asking permission to call Willett for service in arranging the militia in Tryon County. Washington replied that he would be glad to release Willett if General James Clinton could spare him. The Governor wrote to his brother, asking his permission. He also informed Willett of the correspondence and asked him to talk the matter over with General Clinton, adding: "If agreeable to him and yourself, I may have you command one of two militia regiments being raised to defend this frontier."

Marinus Willett received the letter in March. He was in Albany at the time, in a disgruntled mood. A Frenchman, Pierre Regnier, had been given command of a New York regiment of Continentals, though Regnier stood below both Willett and Frederick Weissenfelt in order of preference. It was bad enough to have a foreigner pushed ahead of him. It was an outright insult to offer him the command of a regiment of militia and thus lose rank in the Continental Line.

He wrote Governor Clinton: "The bear Idea of being Lt. Col. Comdt. of a Regiment of Militia, while Lt. Col. Regnier, who stands much lower in the N York line than I do, is Commandant of a Continental Regt in the same State is attended with very disagreeable reactions." He would see Colonel Weissenfelt, who should have had the Regnier appointment. He would accept no other appointment in the interim. If the promotion of Regnier were confirmed he would retire to some business where he "might have an opportunity of free himself of such dissagreable embarrassements." He did not close the door, however. He would ride over to Poughkeepsie to see the Governor after he had conversed with Weissenfelt.

Meanwhile James Clinton had written to his brother, agreeing to release Willett for the Tryon County command but fearing that "unless the dispute between Lt. Cols. Wisenfelts and Regnier, in which he conceives himself interested, should be decided in favor of the former, we shall lose his services altogether, and if otherwise, it is more than likely Regnier will resign, who is a valuable officer."

Willett did not accept the Tryon County command. He remained in the Third New York regiment under Gansevoort, while both Regnier and Weissenfelt gained commands in Clinton's brigade.

George Clinton gave up. He wrote to the distressed Harper that he could not advise the settlers whether to continue on their farms or to remove to the interior. Measures would be taken to protect the Valley from invasion in force. Little could be promised to combat small parties.

The Indians near Onondaga Lake had been a particular menace. Goose Van Schaick, in command at Fort Stanwix, was assigned to the task of intimidating them and Willett was sent up from Albany to assist him.

Willett rode up by way of Fort Johnstown on the tenth of April. The Indians and Tories swooped down on that vicinity the same day, took two prisoners, abused them generally, tried to get information and finally released them. They reported to William Harper, who wrote Governor Clinton: "The Deponant saeth that Sunday, ye 11 instant, about son a hour high in the after nune, he left his house at Fort Johnston to go to the hous whare Wm Harper, Esqr., and Coln Harper dwels, about one mile distante from Fort Johnston, to hear what neus, as he expected that Coln Harper was cum Albany; that he went along the publick rod about one thurd of the way, till he came to a bruck whare he see severall Indens runing towards him, naked with thier guns in thier hands they layed hold of him and tuck the handcurch from his neck, and the buckells out of his knes & shues, & then convayed to the rest of thier party, who Lay at a small distance from the roade." Stephen Lush wrote Clinton that "Colonel Willett passed this Place on his way to Fort Schuyler but about 20 minutes before Inhabitants were taken off." If the colonel had been a half hour later, he might have met with a similar fate; yet again, Willett probably would have found ways and means of escaping.

The necessary force assembled at Fort Stanwix by the middle of April. Sixty Oneidas had arrived a few days before and applied for permission to go on an expedition. Van Schaick saluted them with three pieces of cannon from the fort and told them to be on their way. They disappeared into the forest on an expedition of their own. It was a cold April. Snow fell all the night of the 17th. Bright and early the next morning, despite threatening skies, Van Schaick started out. The batteaux were carried to Wood Creek through a flurry of snowflakes. Ice bordered the narrow stream. Snow lay deep along the shores. The army waded through it, while the batteaux men poled their unwieldy craft down the creek. At Oneida Lake the soldiers had to wait three hours for the batteaux, which arrived at three in the afternoon. It was blowy on the lake, but there could be no pause if the Onondagas were to be taken by surprise. The batteaux rocked with the waves all night. At daybreak the end of the lake hove into sight, but the batteaux were badly scattered, so time was consumed in collecting them. The party struggled through the woods for 14 miles and camped at dark without fires, though the night was cold. They set out at daybreak, marched six miles and halted. A scout discovered the villages on Onondaga Lake. The army hurried forward to find the Indian settlement practically deserted. A few Onondagas skirmished briefly and fled. Fifteen were killed and thirty taken prisoners. Van Schaick stayed eight hours, burning and destroying. From thirty to forty houses were demolished. Horses, pigs and other farm animals were slaughtered. Not a man of Van Schaick's party was killed or wounded.

The party camped on the lake shore that night. The next day they rowed seven miles to an island, where they put in, for Oneida Lake was kicking up in fury, the little white caps threatening to submerge the batteaux. The wind blew hard all night and the next morning and subsided as suddenly as it had begun. The party crossed the lake and advanced up Wood Creek as far as Fish Creek, where they camped for the night. The next day, in a pouring rain which made the snow soft and sloppy, the weary but successful soldiers tramped back to Fort Stanwix, where they were saluted by three pieces of cannon. After the plunder had been distributed, Willett returned to Albany.

In the meantime Congress had decided that something drastic had to be done about the Indian menace. On March 6th General John Sullivan of New Hampshire was appointed by Washington to take command of an expedition against the Iroquois. The main army was to rendezvous at Wyoming and advance by boat and land up the Susquehanna River and be joined at Tioga by a smaller force from the Mohawk Valley under General James Clinton. The latter group was to portage batteaux from Canajoharie to Otsego Lake, row down that body of water and then down the Susquehanna to meet Sullivan. The assembling of such a large body of troops would be slow and laborious. The expedition probably would not be able to accomplish its objective before mid-summer.

Sullivan discovered upon his arrival at Easton in Pennsylvania on May 8th that a tangled wilderness intervened between him and Tioga. A road would have to be cut to Wyoming before the army could march, so he sent a detachment to perform this task. The New Hampshire regiments under General Enoch Poor arrived at Easton "without tents or anything else." An order from Peekskill for 1160 pairs of overalls and 2100 shirts for Colonel Philip Van Cortlandt's Second New Yorkers had not come. The Pennsylvania authorities were slow in procuring wagons, for nothing could be done without the consent of the wagon-masters.

General Sullivan received a letter from Washington: "The expedition you are appointed to command is to be directed against the hostile tribes of the six nations of Indians, with their associates and adherents. The immediate objects are the total destruction and devastation of their settlements and the capture of as many prisoners of every age and sex as possible. It will be essential to ruin their crops now in the ground and prevent their planting more. . . . You will not by any means listen to any overture to peace before the total ruin of their settlements is effected."

Sullivan set about to execute these definite orders to the best of his ability, despite the difficulties which stood in his way. His efforts were mostly on paper. Letters flew thick and fast between Easton and Philadelphia, between Easton and General Washington. The Philadelphia Council, bound round with red tape, were slow in providing the necessary wagons. The road had been cleared to within 23 miles of Wyoming through country "so thick with laurel that a man cannot get through them but on his hands and knees." Beyond that point swamps and sloughs were almost incredible. The clothing problem seemed hopeless. Sullivan wrote Washington: "I think it exceedingly cruel, that those brave Fellows, who must necessarily encounter every hardship incident to war should feel the want of clothing, when those whose Province it is might easily prevent it." Washington wrote back, telling Sullivan to hurry up his operations. The New Hampshire lawyer, taken aback, replied that he had notified General Clinton that he would march "tomorrow" (July 31).

General James Clinton also was having his troubles. The purchasing power of Continental Bills of Credit was at its lowest ebb. Profiteers were taking advantage of the situation; by manipulating prices they were able to sell flour at a dollar a pound. Clinton ordered Walter Livingston, one of the Commissioners, to requisition all wheat, flour and meal in the county of Albany for the use of the army and to deposit it in the manor of Livingston.

Clinton's Brigade consisted of the Third, Fourth and Fifth New York regiments, the Fourth Pennsylvanians, a detachment from the Sixth Massachusetts line, a company from Colonel John Lamb's New York artillery and a handful of volunteers led by Colonel John Harper.

The Third New Yorkers left Albany on June 6th. The boats were transported overland to Schenectady, where they were loaded with three months' supply of provisions. These batteaux were in charge of Henry Glen, Division Quarter Master General, who superintended their loading and sent them up the Mohawk under an armed escort.

The batteaux were flat-bottomed boats about forty feet in length and six feet across in the center. Their ends terminated in points. Each clumsy vessel weighed four and a half tons each and was capable of carrying 1500 pounds of cargo. They were sailed, rowed or poled, according to the strength of the wind and the depth of the river. It was several days before the regiment reached Canajoharie and camped on the flats where Happy Hollow Creek emptied its waters into the Mohawk River. The Canajoharie Flats were the ancient maize land of the Mohawk Indians. They had been cleared of forest and shrubs and the rich grass promised to offer excellent forage for the horses accompanying the expedition. Lieutenant Colonel Pierre Regnier, with his French accent and engaging smile, was there to greet Gansevoort and Willett, for he had been sent up the river with the Commissary to get the camp ready to receive the stores.

A dapper young officer rode up to Willett. He was dressed in a snuff-colored coat, woollen checked shirt and striped trousers. When he doffed his round felt hat, his wig slipped from his head, revealing a bald pate covered with scars. It was Jimmy Gregg returning to the wars after his recovery from his frightful experience at Fort Stanwix. Willett had not expected to see him alive, but here he was, brusque as ever, carrying with him a letter from "dear Caty" to her "dear Peter" and enclosing "a little bag of pepper." Gregg did not go on the Sullivan expedition, but returned to Albany to take charge of forwarding supplies.

General Clinton arrived on June 15th and established his headquarters a mile and a half to the east. Two days later the Fourth Pennsylvanians with 36 batteaux landed at sundown and pitched their tents to the left of the Third New Yorkers. The artillery also pulled in with seven brass pieces. Willett and Regnier took charge of the landing and preparing of the batteaux for the difficult portage to Otsego Lake. Willett had volunteered for this task, which was to be carried on via the King's Highway, which left the Mohawk River one and a half miles west of Canajoharie Creek, followed the south branch of the Happy Hollow Creek and then ran in a westerly direction. An extension of this road had been constructed in 1773 through the valley of Salt Springville to Springfield. This route cut off five miles, was less hilly and was in good condition for the times.

While the batteaux were being prepared, Major Whiting and his Massachusetts troops were marching across from Cherry Valley to take post at the northern end of Otsego Lake, where they would receive the batteaux as they came over the portage and send them down the lake.

Willett had not chosen an easy task. One hundred boats had come in with the Third New Yorkers, 36 more with the Pennsylvanians and 100 more were expected momentarily. Clinton had ordered 300 or 400 wagons to be collected at Canajoharie to transport the batteaux and stores to Otsego Lake. The Tryon County farmers were quick to co-operate. Horses and wagons began to pour in as soon as the first boats landed at Canajoharie. The farmers were anxious to get started and Willett did not miss his opportunity. The heavy batteaux were rolled onto wagons. The provisions, packed carefully, were stowed into several kinds of vehicles. The train began to move over the hills toward Springfield, steadily, unfailingly. Not that there were no difficulties. The road was narrow and many a wheel became enmired in the low places. Curses rent the June air. Much perspiration poured from tanned foreheads, despite the fact that the weather, usually hot at that time of year, remained cool and damp. Willett issued rum generously.

On Sunday the 20th the first train of 60 batteaux arrived at Otsego Lake. The returning wagons were sent back via Sprout Brook, reloaded and started off again on the portage road. Brant's Indians flitted through the forest, watching every move but keeping at a safe distance, for Butler's Rifles were guarding the convoys, and these Pennsylvanians were noted for their accuracy. Five hundred wagons were plying back and forth between the river and the lake. Five teams of horses were used with each wagon. By the end of the week all of the batteaux had been conveyed across the portage, together with the provisions and ammunition. A detachment had been sent to the foot of Otsego Lake to dam up the outlet in order to raise the water of the creek, which emptied into the Susquehanna River. This operation completed, scouts were sent out to break the beaver dams in streams entering the lake, thus adding quantities of water to that body.

When General Clinton arrived at the head of the lake on July 2, he gave a party in celebration of the successful portage. Each officer was given a keg of rum for his men. The 3d was occupied in crossing the lake with the batteaux and provisions. Some of the regiments marched along the shore. The whole brigade camped at the foot of the lake on the night before the fourth of July. The Indians greeted them with shots and yells. Though the sentries fired at the redskins, they kept up their menacing tactics, so that the whole brigade was kept under arms one hour later than usual and the men were sent to their tents with orders not to pull off their clothes. Indian tracks were found near the picket posts the next morning.

General orders were issued for celebrating the anniversary of the Independence of America. The general was pleased to order "that all the Troops under his command should draw a Jill of Rum per Man, extraordinary, in Memory of that Happy Event." Marinus Willett, with a fatigue party of four captains, four subalterns, four sergeants and 200 men set to work to clear a parade ground in front of the camp. They worked two hours, slashing at the low bushes with axes, carrying the brush to piles where it could be dried and burned. At three-thirty General Clinton's brigade was drawn up in review, with Butler and Weissenfelt on the left, Gansevoort and Dubois on the right, and the artillery on the two wings. A *feu de joie* was rolled across the lake; it echoed and re-echoed from the green hills. Rev. John Gano preached a sermon on the text: "This day shall be a memorial unto you throughout your generation." The remainder of the day was given over to merriment.

At the close of this happy anniversary, Lieut. Erkuries Beatty of the Fourth Pennsylvanians told his diary: "This day three year being the day that Independence was declared it was celebrated by firing a Feu De Joy all the troops was drew up on the banks of the lake in one line with the two pieces of artillery on the right there was 13 pieces of cannon fired and three volleys of musquetry one after the other and three cheers with every fire it was done extraordinary well with great exactness, afterwards the troops was drew up in a circle by colums on a little hill when Parson Granoo preached us a sermon suitable to the occasion from the 4 chapter of Exodus and 12 verse, afterwards the troops was dismissed. Col. Rignier Adjt. Gen. gave an invitation to all the officers to come and drink Grog with him in the evening accordingly a number of officers (almost all) assembled at a large Bowry which he had prepared on the bank of the lake, but however we sot on the ground in a large circle and closed the day with a number of Toast suitable a great deal of Mirth for two or three hours and then retired to our tents, the whole day conducted extremely well considering the place, a great deal of provision came over the Lake here today—weather very warm."

General Clinton wrote to his brother that 208 boats, all stores, provisions and baggage of the army had arrived safely at the foot of the lake, and that he "was convinced that such a quantity of each hath never before been transported over so bad a Road in so short a time and with less accidents, so that I am now in the most readiness to move down the Susquehanna whenever I receive General Sullivan's orders for that purpose."

Marinus Willett had done his work well, as usual.

Clinton was ready, but there was no word from Sullivan. Time was spent drilling the men. The drums and fifes were ordered to practice together every day in order that a more uniform mode of playing be adopted throughout the brigade. The weather was ill-suited to drilling, for frequent storms and high winds blew in from the lake, raising havoc with the tents. Cool nights caused complaining among the soldiers, who had insufficient bedding. The practice of swimming in the middle of the day was prejudicial to the health of the men; it was to be discontinued immediately. Dysentery struck the camp. A number of "necessary holes" were dug in the most convenient places for the regiments, "which are to be covered every Morning and if any Soldier is found easing himself at any other Place, he shall be severely punished."

A soldier of the Massachusetts line dropped dead while rolling a keg of provisions. Several deserters were caught; one of them received 100 lashes, while another was executed. The Indians threatened the German Flatts. Colonel Gansevoort made a hurried march up the Mohawk to discover that it was a false alarm. There was also good news. Mad Anthony Wayne had stormed Stony Point successfully.

The officers felt the strain. An old feud broke out between Colonel Dubois and Captain Jansen. It all dated back to a drinking-bout in Albany in 1775. Jansen, in the cups, had passed the remark that Dubois was a horse-thief, that he had been known to have stolen three horses while in Canada with Montgomery, and that he had given one of them to George Clinton to cover matters up. In 1777 at Schoharie there had been a renewal of hostilities which had been quelled only by the intervention of the Governor himself. Jansen had considered the affair closed but Dubois, through slips of the tongue, had spread news behind Jansen's back; and the captain, on the parade ground, had called the colonel a rascal and a liar. Jansen was arrested and allowed to cool his heels in the guard tent for two weeks, during which time he wrote a lengthy vindication of his actions. Dubois, laughing up his sleeve, said Jansen had forced his own arrest to avoid a challenge to a duel. He also felt that the captain was beneath his notice.

The affair was aired at a Court of Inquiry on August 5th. Colonel Willett sat as Judge Advocate. The Court decided that Colonel Dubois stood acquitted of Jansen's charges, that Jansen was deceived in his information about Dubois, and that, in view of Jansen's character, the colonel should withdraw his arrest. All animosities between the two officers were to be extinguished.

Sullivan's letter arrived that same day, ordering Clinton to march on the 9th to make a junction with the main army at Tioga. This news the general chose to withhold, though the men were restless and unruly. John Gano, the chaplain who guided the spiritual life of the brigade, went to see Clinton on Saturday to inform him of the dissatisfaction in the ranks. Clinton told Gano the army would march on Monday, but that nothing must be said until the regimental orders were issued on Sunday night. Gano preached a sermon from the text: "Be ready to depart on the morrow." Clinton, outwitted, announced after the service that the army would break camp at sunrise.

Marinus Willett commanded the troops that went by land, he also having charge of the cattle and horses. After their long idleness at the lake, the troops were ebullient and unruly. The woods abounded in rattlesnakes and the men made quite a pastime of taking pot-shots at them with their muskets. Orders had to be issued to restrain the men from firing. The weather continued hot and sultry. Outside Unadilla the soldiers stopped to gather raspberries and to make a huge quantity of punch which enlivened their spirits. They also halted frequently to bathe in the Susquehanna, usually choosing spots where the cooks were ladling out water for their kettles. An order was issued to the advantage of the cooks. Willett must have felt relief when the troops reached Unadilla and he was assigned to the boats.

A few days later the Clinton brigade encountered General Poor and 1500 men whom Sullivan had sent from Tioga to meet them. The troops marched in a heavy rain to Tioga, where the army was encamped on a peninsula where the Susquehanna met the Cayuta Creek. Sullivan had been there several days. One skirmish had been fought at Chemung; the Indians had been routed and their village burned. Clinton's arrival was greeted by a discharge of thirteen cannon.

The expedition started toward the Indian country on the morning of August 26th. It was a splendid array. The first brigade consisted of four New Jersey regiments, with Brigadier General Maxwell in charge. Colonel Willett, because of his knowledge of the Indians and the New York countryside, was transferred to this brigade. Inasmuch as Clinton's brigade was to bring up the rear, one can easily imagine Willett's elation at this transfer.

The Jersey troops wore blue coats faced with red, with their regimental numbers stamped boldly on the pewter buttons. Proudest among them were Littell's Jersey Blues, who boasted blue breeches and light blue stockings. Others wore overalls dipped in blue dye.

Poor's three New Hampshire regiments formed the second brigade, together with Major Whiting and his detachment from the Sixth Massachusetts line. The New Hampshire troops were arrayed in sky-blue coats faced with scarlet and lined with white. Their waistcoats were of buckskin and their white stockings of gray wool. The Massachusetts men wore blue regimentals faced with white, green waistcoats and white leggings. Some of them, having been long at Cherry Valley, favored hunting shirts and overalls.

The Pennsylvanians under General Edward Hand marched next. Their brown coats had buff facings; buff leggings and breeches completed their attire. They carried their rifles in a peculiarly erect manner. With them marched a group of Morgan's Riflemen, drab in their hunting costumes. Among the Pennsylvanians was Lieutenant Thomas Boyd, who would never return.

The Second New Yorkers under Van Cortlandt joined Clinton's brigade. These men wore light brown coats faced with blue. The Fourth New Yorkers also favored brown, while Gansevoort's regiment was still dressed in gray with green facings. Lamb's artillery, clad in blue faced with buff, brought up the rear.

The brigades marched in squares, protecting their flanks with scouts, for lurking Indians had scalped two of Sullivan's men while they were waiting at Tioga for Clinton to arrive. The men were also ordered to be careful with their rifles, for hadn't a careless youth shot Captain Kimball only a few days before? The funeral had been a sad affair, for Kimball, a veteran of five campaigns, had been well-liked.

Rains had swelled the rivers. A whole day was spent cutting a way through a narrow defile so that the artillery and provisions could be brought through. Time was spent laying waste the fields and cutting down the fruit trees at Chemung. The soldiers also gorged themselves on fresh vegetables.

Rumors flew that Colonel Butler and his Tories had formed a junction with the Indians and were waiting to intercept Sullivan's army. A scout from Hand's brigade came in shortly before noon on the 28th with the news that a breastwork made of pine logs covered with green scrub bushes had been erected on rising ground commanding the road along which the Continentals were marching. At that point there was a bend in the river, which crossed the road and then turned to the right, parallel with the breastwork. A strong enemy party was posted on the hill 150 yards to the rear of the breastwork.

Sullivan acted quickly. Poor was sent to encircle the hill and fall upon the enemy's rear. Clinton was to sustain Poor. Maxwell was to keep in close column to attack whenever

Poor attained his objective. The skirmish was short. A cannonade from in front plus Poor's attack in the rear caused the enemy to flee in disorder, leaving a dozen dead and a great number of packs, blankets, arms and Indian jewels. Two prisoners were taken, one a Tory, the other a Negro. From them Sullivan learned that both Butlers, Brant and McDonald had been in the skirmish with five white companies. The American loss was three killed and 39 wounded. The latter were sent back to Tioga.

The party pushed on. A day was spent at Catherine's, destroying cornfields and fruit trees. The town of 30 houses was burned. By the fifth of September, the army reached Appletown, where 13 houses were burned and a large orchard destroyed. Some of the houses were of hewed timbers; one had a chimney. It was here that the soldiers saw three tombs of Indian chiefs, "painted fine and covered with bark."

Sullivan had orders to destroy the Indian settlements. He obeyed them to the letter. Villages were burned, apple trees girdled, vegetable crops destroyed. By the middle of September the expedition had swept up Seneca Lake and was approaching the chief Seneca castle. The Tories and Indians had caused no trouble after the skirmish at Newtown. Now they made their last attempt at harassing the invaders. A scouting party of 27 men under Lieutenant Thomas Boyd was ambushed. Eleven men came back to tell that the remainder of the party had been killed or captured.

The Genesee Valley lay clothed in the glory of autumn. Grass six to ten feet high covered the ground. The trees on the rolling hills were red, yellow and brown. Wild grapes grew profusely along the rough road. Gardens were filled with ripe vegetables. The soldiers ate their fill.

The Seneca castle stood on the west bank of the Genesee River, which ran swiftly along, offering little chance for easy fording. The men crossed in platoons, their arms locked together to lend mutual support. They staggered up the steep rise on the other side and stopped to catch their breaths. They had reached Chenondanah, the western door to the Iroquois Long House.

Elation turned to gloom, for at Little Beard's Town they found the bodies of Boyd and a sergeant, both with the heads cut off. Boyd had been brutally tortured. He had been skinned, his back badly knifed, his nails pulled out. A knife projected from the sergeant's mutilated body. The facts of the case came out later. "Having been denuded, Boyd was tied to a sapling, where the Indians first practiced on the steadiness of his nerves by hurling their tomahawks apparently at his head, but so as to strike the trunk of the sapling as near to his head as possible without hitting it, groups of Indians, in the meantime, brandishing their knives and dancing around him with the most frantic demonstrations of joy. His nails were pulled out, his nose cut off, and one of his eyes plucked out. His tongue was also cut out, and he was stabbed in various places. After amusing themselves sufficiently in this way, a small incision was made in his abdomen, and the end of one of his intestines taken and fastened to a tree. The victim was then unbound, and driven around the tree by brute force, until his intestines had all been literally drawn from his body and wound around its trunk. His sufferings were terminated by striking his head from his body." The bodies of Boyd and the sergeant were buried at the foot of a wild plum tree at the junction of two creeks.

There were happier incidents. A white woman who had been taken by the Indians at Wyoming joined the Americans. An old Indian squaw, left behind because she was too feeble to accompany her tribe in its flight, was spared. And a little boy was found, nearly starved. He was adopted by Captain Thomas Machin.

The Seneca castle was laid in ruins. The whole army was ordered out for this task of devastation. Two thirds of the men worked, while the remainder stood guard. Of the vast fields of ripened corn, a supply was kept for the returning army, while the rest was destroyed. The orchards were laid waste, many of the trees being girdled to save time.

Sullivan divided his forces. Gansevoort and a detachment of 100 men were sent back to the Mohawk Valley to chastise the Mohawks and burn their castles. Others swept down the east shore of Seneca Lake, burning and plundering. They met with no opposition. By the end of September the troops were back at Tioga, enjoying the special rations of rum handed out to them.

Marinus Willett did not go with Gansevoort. He returned with the main army to Easton, arriving on October 17th. His opinion of the Sullivan expedition was never recorded. In writing the story of his military career, the lanky colonel merely mentioned that he was part of that plundering army. What he thought of it all, no one will ever know, but from remarks he made in later life it may be assumed that he was not in full accord with the policy of devastation advocated by Washington and pursued so conscientiously by Sullivan. Willett believed that the best way to deal with Indians was to flatter them, not to stir them to vengeance by destroying their villages. After the war he was destined to perform one act of conciliation and to refuse to be part of another army which waged war against the Ohio Indians.

The army marched from Easton to Pompton, where the hungry soldiers raised havoc with the inhabitants. They slipped from camp and stole everything in sight, being particularly partial to hen-roosts. Firm orders had to be issued in an attempt to keep them from plundering. A severe drought had prevented the mills from running, so flour was a scarce article. So the soldiers kept right on stealing horses, hogs, sheep and poultry. Willett sat as Judge in several courts martial involving these soldiers. He was probably glad when the army went into winter quarters near Morristown on December 6th.

During that winter he led two raids on the British. He and 500 men crossed over to Staten Island on the ice and captured 17 Wagonloads of stores, including sugar, butter and gin. Later on he led an expedition to Paulus Hook and drove away British cattle.

“The Devil” Takes Over

THE SULLIVAN EXPEDITION HAD SUCCEEDED in destroying the Indian settlements and cutting off supplies of grain and vegetables from the British army, but it also had instilled into the Indians a feeling of resentment which led to renewed atrocities in 1780. Cherry Valley was wiped out of existence on April 26th. Eight settlers were killed and fourteen carried into captivity. In May Sir John Johnson led 500 British, Tories and Indians into the Mohawk Valley. His objective was Johnson Hall, where he hoped to remove treasures which he had buried there before his hasty flight to Canada several years before. He also wished to wreak vengeance on those Whigs who had forced his withdrawal from the Valley. He recovered his valuables and 20 slaves, and his Tories and Indians left death and devastation in their wake. The Oneidas abandoned their villages, which were totally destroyed, while the Indians took refuge in Schenectady. Gansevoort and his regiment were ordered to escort batteaux loaded with supplies to Fort Stanwix. They had no sooner left Fort Plain when Joseph Brant swooped down on the settlers, who were busy harvesting. Fifty-three dwellings were burned, 16 settlers were murdered and about 60 captured.

In October Johnson came from Oswego, passed to the west of the settlements and met Brant near the Susquehanna River. Many Tories joined the party, after having been promised eight dollars for each scalp they lifted. They swept up the

Schoharie Valley, burning and plundering. Major Woolsey, in command in that area, would have surrendered had not Timothy Murphy fired at the British flag which was approaching the fort accompanied by an officer in green and a fifer and drummer playing "Yankee Doodle." Woolsey gave way to Colonel Vrooman, who succeeded in holding the three Schoharie forts but was unable to prevent the invaders from destroying great quantities of hay and grain which had been stored in mills, barns and stacks for the winter.

Johnson's troops met the Mohawk River at Fort Hunter, which they passed without attacking and advanced up the south bank. Brant and his men crossed the river and proceeded up the north shore. Both parties continued their plundering.

General Robert Van Rensselaer, with the finest body of troops ever to be assembled in Albany, started west after sending orders to Colonel John Brown at Fort Paris and Colonel John Harper at Fort Plain to hold out. Brown was to attack the enemy in front the next morning, while Van Rensselaer fell upon their rear. Between them they would encircle and crush the entire Johnson party. Colonel Brown, whose courage was proverbial, attacked Johnson in an open field near Stone Arabia. Outnumbered and outflanked, he was forced to retreat. Brown was killed, scalped and left lying on the field clad only in his ruffled shirt. Johnson passed on up the river, burning two churches at Stone Arabia and innumerable dwellings, while the inhabitants fled to the woods.

Van Rensselaer reached Fort Hunter at daybreak, where he was joined by the Schoharie militia. Colonel Harper and his men from Fort Plain were added to the party a short distance up the Mohawk, near the spot where Brant had crossed the river. Firing could be heard ahead. An advance party under Capt. Robert McKean crossed the river, but Van Rensselaer did not support it. The sun indicated the approach of noon and the general was hungry, so he went to Fort Plain to eat dinner with Governor Clinton, who had accompanied the army. After eating he advanced leisurely to Fort Herkimer, where he sent an advance party after the enemy. This group marched several miles, contacted the rear-guard of Johnson's party and halted to wait for support. News came that Van Rensselaer had tired of the chase and was returning to Albany.

The militia of Tryon County, who had flocked to Van Rensselaer's banner, eager to strike a decisive blow at the enemy, returned disheartened and disgusted. If this was the kind of leadership Albany was to send them, what chance did they have of coping with Johnson and Brant? They were particularly disgruntled because this general had given his name to Fort Plain. Agitation against Van Rensselaer forced a Court of Inquiry at Albany, but it is said that the general was acquitted because of his wealth and social position.

Settlers were leaving the Mohawk Valley. Of what use was it to hold out now, with the Tories and Indians coming every month to destroy the product of their hard-won labors? Another campaign would see the end of American enterprise west of Albany. Even that city might fall to the enemy. Something had to be done to prevent this catastrophe and done quickly. In the winter of 1780-1781 the state decided to raise two levies of troops for the protection of the Mohawk Valley. Troops were all right, but of what use were they without an able commander?

There was only one possible choice—Marinus Willett. His name was a tower of strength in the Valley. With the reorganization of the army in January, the lanky colonel had been discharged from command of the Fifth New York regiment. In April the command of one of the two new militia regiments was offered to Willett, the command of the other to his friend, Frederick Weissenfelt. Willett was not too pleased with the offer. Ranks in the state regiments were lower than those in the Continental Line. If he accepted this difficult chore, he might lose forever any chance of advancement in the regular army. But it was obvious that the Valley wanted him. Dominie Gros was agitating for his acceptance. The officer in charge at Fort Plain was indolent and unpopular. His sons were suspected of selling arms and ammunition to the enemy. Fort Plain should be commanded by an officer of ability. Colonel Willett was universally looked upon in that light. Pressure was put to bear on Willett. He accepted the command.

Governor Clinton informed him on April 28th that the regiment would be made up of levies from Albany, Tryon, Charlotte and Dutchess Counties. Willett was ordered to select his place of rendezvous and to accept only able-bodied men fit for active service, completely armed and provided agreeable to law. He was to settle his private affairs and take a seat somewhere in Tryon County.

Difficulties complicated Willett's task at the outset. Colonel John Blair refused to send any men, he having formed an alliance with Vermont in that section's dispute with New York. Tryon County sent 60 men and Albany County 400. Charlotte County did not send a man. By the end of the month of May 470 men had been mustered, but over 100 had deserted.

Willett assigned the 348 men left to him as follows: Saratoga 79, Ballston 15, Johnstown 61, German Flatts 69, Canajoharie 53, Fort Hunter 29, Schoharie 11, Catskill 22 and Albany 9. It was a meagre force with which to man the twenty forts between Schenectady and the German Flatts.

The outpost where Willett had made his reputation was no more. His friend, Robert Cochran, had been in command of Fort Stanwix. In May heavy rains had almost ruined the works. Provisions were low. The soldiers became lazy and careless. They were playing ball one day at noon when a fire was discovered. It gained headway rapidly; despite the frantic efforts of Cochran and the garrison, every barrack was consumed. They managed to save the magazine and a portion of the provisions. George Clinton was furious. He couldn't see how a fire could break out at noon after days of heavy rain. He suspected that it was no mere accident. Cochran was to shelter the troops the best he could and send the women and children down the river by boat. A week later Cochran received orders to abandon Fort Stanwix.

The ammunition and supplies were brought to Fort Herkimer, which became the frontier outpost. Marinus Willett rode up there with Dominie Gros. His task would be difficult. The Valley was harassed by enemies who were artful as well as cruel. Scouts would have to be kept out at all times. Extreme vigilance and perseverence would have to be exercised. Constant contact between forts would be necessary. The green troops would have to be trained and disciplined. Desertion would be frequent; all effort would have to be made to prevent these escapes from the ranks and severe punishment would be the lot of captured offenders.

Marinus Willett penned a long letter to General Washington, explaining to his hero the situation as he saw it: "I am in this county by order of Governor Clinton. Among other particulars in a set of instructions I have received from him, are the following clawses. 'For a variety of reasons, I conceive it will conduce most to the good of the service that you should take post yourself in Tryon County. In the distribution of the troops, you are to have regard to the aid to be derived from the Continental troops, and militia; to whom I will give such orders as will enable you to avail yourself of their aid.'

"In consequence of these orders, and in expectations of the Legislatures making provision to execute a plan That given a sketch of to Governor Clinton, I am at present on these frontiers; Impeled by the situation of things in these parts, I beg leave to lay before your Excellency a short description of this

County with its present state. It is a Country of the most Luxuriant soil. Not only the lands along the river are exceeding rich but the whole body of the back lands are of the first quality, exceeding in general any tract of Country I passed through in our march upon the western expedition under General Sullivan. Most of the settlements lay along or not far back of the Mohawk river. At the commencement of the present war both sides of the river from Schenectida to Germantown which is seventy miles the settlements were considerably thick and every thing had the appearance of ease and plenty. There were besides several valuable farms extending Fifteen miles higher up the river than Germantown. Which is however the last place were any number of famalies had fixed themselves together. The militia of the county at that time did not amount to less than two Thousand five hundred men. In such a Country blessed with so fine a soil lying along a delightfull river which affordeed an easy Transportation of the produce to a valuable market with a Climate exceeded by none, it might have been expected a population would taken place. But this was stagnated by means which you are undoubtedly well acquainted with. Those obstructions will I hope in a little time be removed and this part of the world which is itself one of the first places perhaps on this continent may expect to be passed by none. Flourish it must. Nothing but the hand of Tyrany can prevent it much longer from becoming the garden of America. The place from which I now write is at present the advance settlement up the river, and lays sixty three miles from Schenectida. This strip of sixty miles in length is liable to Indian Incurtions on both sides of the river, which the inhabitants have frequently experienced, and so severe has been their experience that at present out of two thousand five hundred men which at the Commencement of the war had upon their militia roles, Their whole number of Classable Inhabitants does not amount to twelve hundred. By a law of the

State every male person not being a slave who was above sixteen years of age is to be numbered into Classes. The Individuals of each Class are respectively to pay as much towards raising men for the publick service as they may be assessed by persons a pointed by the Class for that purpose. These are what I mean by Classable Inhabitants, of these sort of men there being not twelve hundred, the number liable to be called upon to do militia Duty, will hardly exceed Eight hundred, so that there is a reduction in the County of at least two thirds, since the commencement of the war. Of these two thirds I dont think I shall give a very wild account if I say, that one third of them have been killed, or carried captive by the enemy; one third have been removed into the Interiour parts of the Country, And one third Deserted to the enemy . . . The Present distressed situation of the Inhabitants is such as to demand sympathy from the most unfeeling heart. Every neighbourhood have erected for themselves a fortification, Some of which are made sufficient to evince the truth of an old saying 'That necessity is the mother of Invention.' Within these Forts the Inhabitants in general have taken up their residence. They contain from ten to upwards of fifty famalies in a Fort. and There are twenty-four of these Fortifications within the county. Pitiable indeed is the case of a People thus situated. But wretched as their sutuations are such is the state of the country and such are the People who inhabit it. That should they be fortunate enough to preserve the grane they at present have in the ground they will have an Immence quantity more than will be sufficient for their own consumption.

"To protect this country as much as possible is our present business, and this is the point, to which alone I mean to request your Excellencies attention. By withdrawing the regular troops the county is undoubtedly much weakened. At this time I have not in the whole Country more than two hundred and fifty men exclusive of the militia. Some reignforsments Governor Clinton writes me are coming from the Eastward. These we may hope will come part this way, and by others being sent to the northward, I flatter myself I shall be able to withdraw that part of the levies under my command and which are at present that way.

"I heartily wish to have as much force as possible, to assist in the preservation of a people whose sufferings have already been so exceedingly great. But be the force larger or smaller I can only promise to do everything in my power for the relief of a people of whom I had some knowledgee in their prosperous days And am now acquainted with in the time of their great distress A people whose case I most sincerely commiserate. At the same time I think it my Duty to Inform your Excellency, That after withdrawing the two regular regiments from these parts I expect to have the command of all the troops that may be ordered into this county for its common defence and that the internal direction and distribution will be comited to my care. This is what Governor Clinton told me would be the case and should the Legislature make such further provision for the defence of the county, as I have requested notwithstanding its present deplorable situation I shall hope to have the force of the county much more respectable than hitherto it has been. Nor shall I exceed my hopes if in the course of less than twelve months I shall be able to convince the enemy that they are not without their vulnarable Quarters in Western parts of this World.

"Since I have been in this part of the Country, I have been endeavouring to put matters in some kind of a regular train. With the approbation of the Governor I have fixed my Quarters at Canajoharia on account of its Central position And my intention is to manage business so as to have an opportunity of acquainting myself as well as possible with every officer and soldier I may have in charge. In order the better to do this I propose as far as I can make it any way convenient to guard the defirent posts by detachments, to be relieved as the nature of the case will admit, And as the relieved troops will always return to Fort Rensselaer were my Quarters will be I shall have an opportunity of seeing them in their turn all the troops under my Command. The having troops marching backwards and forwards through the Country and frequently changing their routs will answer several purposes, such as will be easily perceived by you Sir, without my mentioning of them. This is not the only way by which I expect to become particularly acquainted with the troops and their situation. The better to enable me to rectify such mistakes as are common among the kind of troops I have at present in charge I shall occasionally visit every part of the country as well for this purpose as for becoming better acquainted with and observing the condition of the militia, upon whose aid I shall be under the necessaty of placing considerable reliance.

"In order to shew that I have some reason to place depence upon the militia I shall first mention a transaction that took place a few nights ago at Canajoharia. An account was sent me at one o'clock in the morning that about fifty Indians and Tories were in the neighbourhood of a place six miles off. Having no troops at the place but a sufficiency for the guards I sent for a Captain of the militia and in less than an hour he was out with seventy men in search of the enemy. In short they are a people who having experienced no Inconsiderable portion of British barbarism, are become keen for revenge and appear properly determined.

"It is with regret I trespass upon your time in this manner, but I am desirous of giving you as good a sketch as I can of the situation of this Country. It is easy for you to perceive that the strength we now have this way is Inadequate to the erecting of the Fortress intended to be built at this place by Major Villafranch the engineer who was ordered here for the purpose of Fortifying this place. Nor did I see the great necessity of such works being erected here. I humbly conceive that some small Improvements as to the works we already have will answer our present purpose. And I am pretty clear it will be all that we shall be able to accomplish. After taking up this representation of our State I should be glad to know your pleasure and every thing within my reach shall be done to perform it.

"If it should meet with your approbation I should be glad to make such a disposition of the cannon and other Ordinance Stores, as may appear most secure and best calculated to protect the Country. For to me it is clear that the way to protect these parts is in case the enemy should again appear this way with any thing of force to Collect all the strength we can get to a point and endeavour to beat them in the field as the enemy may approach the Country through diferent ways without halting to invest any particular place unless they Choose. It is therefore in my opinion by joining our whole force together and beating the enemy out of the country and not defending any one post that we are to endeavour to protect these frontiers—Whilst these small Stockade Forts and Blockhouses which the Inhabitants themselves have erected are in general sufficient to cover them against such parties of Indians and Tories as usually make their appearance this way.

"I should count myself happy in having your sentiments upon this subject. At present I have at this place only one hundred men. Nor is it possible without putting the inhabitants below in general upon the wing to afford this place more men untill I receive some reighforcsments. I need not say to you Sir, that nothing can be done towards erecting the new Fort with the men I now have. I shall therefore only endeavour to repair the works already at this place until I shall receive further orders."

Fort Plain

MARINUS WILLETT RODE SLOWLY from Fort Herkimer to Fort Plain. Here was a country, by his own admission, superior in fertility to the fabulous Genesee lands he had helped to desolate two summers before. Some of the clearings were deserted; blackened timbers raised desolate fingers to indicate spots from where happiness had been driven away. Trees lay prone, waiting for the axe to lop off their drying branches. Crows cawed over fields where no maize had been planted and winged away, disappointed. The fear of Brant and the Butlers had placed a hand of doom on the Mohawk Valley.

Some brave souls had not run away. German farmers labored in the fields between the highroad and the river. The hay stood tall and ripe. If it could be cut and protected there would be enough fodder, not only for the animals of the inhabitants and the protecting soldiery, but a surplus which could be sent down the river to the Grand Army. Now that "The Devil" had been sent to protect them the farmers worked with enthusiasm. They had confidence in Marinus Willett. He would not hesitate to attack the enemy.

Fort Rensselaer, which crowned a plateau overlooking the winding river, was an irregular quadrangle extending along the brow of the steepest slope. The bastions at each corner were constructed of earth and logs; they assumed the appearance of small blockhouses. A hundred yards from the fort, commanding the northern side of the plateau, stood an octagonal blockhouse which was the pride and joy of the settlers. To Willett's practiced eye it was a top-heavy atrocity. One gale of wind would topple it over. Willett smiled. Some day he'd haul out a six-pounder and take a pot-shot at this eyesore. He'd bet a guinea the shot would go right through the damned blockhouse.

All was comfortable inside the fort. The long barracks were ample for the garrison. There were quarters for the officers and a special marquee for the commandant. A small blockhouse in the center of the enclosure could be defended if the parapets were surmounted by the enemy or the strong gates forced. Two apple trees loaded with ripening fruit lent a homey atmosphere unexpected in a frontier fort.

Fort Rensselaer had seen little activity since spring. The officers and soldiers were drinking too much of the popular beverages of the time: flip, made of beer brewed from malt and hops, to which sugar and liquor were added and the whole concoction heated with a hot iron, was more than a mere nightcap; kill-devil, substituting cider for beer, was a favorite for officers' toasts. Some of the officers were veterans of several years' standing; they resented discipline and were prone to fill the night air with boasts and songs, despite repeated orders from Willett to keep silent after tattoo.

The settlers had a grievance. They were willing to endure barbarity and massacre but they resented the fact that their fort had been named after the officer who had behaved so badly the previous year. Fort Plain was good enough for them; they had named it from the view that could be obtained of all the surrounding countryside. They refused to use the name of the Dutchman from Albany who had disgraced the Valley with what they considered craven behavior at Stone Arabia. Willett agreed with the people but he also had to satisfy his superiors at Poughkeepsie, so he used the name Fort Rensselaer in his Regimental Order Book and on letters and documents, except when he was in a hurry.

Several letters written by the colonel at critical moments were headed "Fort Plain." And it is reasonable to assume that he used the local name in dealings with his neighbors, for he had no respect for the name of Robert Van Rensselaer. He hated laggards.

He had little time to worry over these affairs. He had been at Fort Plain exactly two days when the first blow fell. Capt. Lawrence Gros with a scouting party was reconnoitering south toward New Dorlach and New Rhinebeck, settlements suspected of Tory sentiments. He came across the trail of a party of Tories and Indians which he estimated at 500 men. He hustled two mounted men to Fort Plain. They came galloping up the rise as the signal-gun sounded from the blockhouse at Currytown.

Willett sent a messenger post haste to Fort Paris, asking Vedder to collect all troops possible and to advance in forced marches toward the enemy's camp. He rounded up what remained of his garrison and sent a hurry call for the militia. Farmers left their haying and grabbed their muskets.

A bedraggled, wounded man staggered up to Willett. He was Jacob Dievendorf, a Currytown farmer. He had been working in the fields with his two sons and a Negro boy. The Indians had surprised them. There had been no time to rush to the woods at the signal gun. His sons had been killed and scalped, he feared. The Bellingers and the Moyers had been either killed or taken. Old man Putnam had been murdered and scalped. Houses were burning and the Indians were scouring the woods, barking their scalp-yells.

Willett gave the order to march. As his army passed Fort Clyde he picked up the few men that could be spared from that outpost. Night came upon them, but they pushed forward. They found Gros and his forty men at Bowman's Creek. The whole company, hastily counted, numbered less than 200 men. The enemy had over twice that number, but Willett ordered an advance through the tangled underbrush, resting on the assurance that the scouts knew every inch of the territory through which they were passing. They reached a cedar swamp at daybreak and came upon the enemy camp. The men were cooking a breakfast they would never eat.

Willett rejected a frontal attack. The enemy could be conquered only through stratagem. If a small group could detract the Tories and Indians from the movements of the main body, there was a chance of success. It certainly was worth trying, so Willett sent several men over the ridge to show themselves to the enemy. The ruse worked. The Tories and Indians picked up their weapons and chased the skirmishers, who fled toward the ambuscade Willett had prepared for their reception. The yelling Indians were greeted with a deadly fire from behind trees and stumps. A running fight ensued. Indians, Tories and Americans fell. One stump caused the pioneers considerable trouble until a soldier leaned his gun on the shoulder of a comrade and scored a center shot. The stump was silenced.

Marinus Willett stayed in the thick of the fighting, lending encouragement, shouting orders. He held his hat in his hand, remarking that he would catch in it all the balls the enemy could send. At the climax of the struggle he yelled in a loud voice, "My men, stand your ground and I'll bring up the levies and we'll surround the damned rascals!" The enemy, suspecting that they had encountered a superior force, turned tail and ran in all directions.

Capt. Robert McKean led the pursuit, running from tree to tree, shouting and encouraging his men. A bullet caught him. He toppled forward on his face. His son, rushing to his father's assistance, was shot through the mouth. Two other skirmishers lay motionless behind stumps.

Willett came to the stump which had caused so much trouble. A soldier pointed to a pool of blood which was soaking into the leaves, whereupon the colonel remarked laconically, "One that stood behind that stump will never get back to Canada."

They found the enemy camp deserted. Much equipage had been left behind. Articles that were useful were gathered up by the pursuing forces.

Willett halted his men. It would be suicide to rush into the forest after the Indians, so the victorious party marched back to Fort Plain, laden with plunder. They also bore with them four dead comrades and several wounded men, among them the gallant McKean, who was taken in a litter to Capt. Van Alstyne's fortified house.

Vedder and his troops from Fort Paris met the returning party. Willett dispatched them to Currytown to estimate the damage and to bring in any wounded settlers that could be found. Vedder returned to report that all the houses and barns had been destroyed except the holdings of a Tory. Young Jacob Dievendorf had been found alive, half-buried in a pile of dead leaves into which he had crawled after he had been scalped. One of Vedder's men, thinking that an Indian lurked there, had levelled his musket to shoot, but it had been knocked out of his hands by a fellow soldier. Jacob's brother, Frederick, a lad of fourteen, also had been scalped. After lying insensible for several hours, he had revived sufficiently to crawl to the blockhouse. Both boys were covered with blood. One of Vedder's men carried the lifeless figure of a little girl who had died on the way back to Fort Plain. Several others had been taken captive by the Indians. It was feared that they had been murdered and left in the woods.

Capt. McKean died the next day and was buried with military honors in the soldiers' graveyard a short distance from the fort. His loss was a severe one for, in addition to being an excellent Indian fighter, he had been popular with all men at the fort. His son recovered, as did the Dievendorf boys. A German physician from Stone Arabia did the best he could with the wounded. He had no rum with which to bathe the wounds, for the two barrels consigned to Fort Plain had been intercepted somewhere in the Valley by a regiment of Continentals, who had put the liquor to what they thought a better use. Willett sent the wounded to Schenectady, for there was no surgeon at Fort Plain and intercourse between that place and the German Flatts was so hazardous that Dr. Petrie could not come down from Fort Dayton.

Two men appeared from New Dorlach, a Tory stronghold, bearing a letter stating that there had been great firing down their way. Willett did not like the looks of the messengers, so he put them in the guardhouse, where they made confessions involving the people of New Dorlach. Willett ordered a detachment to New Dorlach, where they broke up the settlement and brought in ninety head of cattle for use at Fort Plain.

Willett's victory over Dockstader and his Tories and Indians was received with enthusiasm from Albany to the German Flatts. "The Devil" became a conquering hero to the German settlers, who went back to their haying with renewed confidence. The City of Albany, which had been living in imminent fear of attack from the west, congratulated Willett and his men and presented the colonel with the freedom of the city.

Willett's reply to this honor was characteristic of the soldier: "I beg leave to offer you my warmest acknowledgments for your favorable sentiments of the conduct of the few gallant officers and soldiers engaged with me in the late action in Tryon County. This mark of your approbation must essentially increase the satisfaction they have already experienced of being instrumental in chastising a cruel and savage enemy, (the natural ally of the British King), and will afford a rich compensation for the toils and difficulties they had to encounter.

"I esteem myself much honored by your resolution of this date, and particularly by being admitted to the rights of a freeman in this ancient and respectable city. Be pleased to accept my thanks for your politeness on this occasion, and permit me at the same time to observe to you, gentlemen, that I wish never to sheath the sword I have early drawn in defence of American *liberty*, as long as there is a soldier or a savage in the service of Britain, in any part of the States of America."

News of other attacks reached Fort Plain. Donald McDonald, a Tory from Johnstown, had taken two sons of Christian Schell near Fort Dayton and had been wounded and captured. At Stone Arabia three Shults boys had been at work in the fields along with a Negro boy. They had stacked their arms against a tree near the edge of the clearing. Stealthy Indians had seized the weapons, rendering the workers helpless. All four had been taken into captivity. And Schoharie had been raided again quite successfully. There was something wrong at Schoharie. Willett did not know just what, but he was disgusted and discouraged.

He wrote Governor Clinton a long letter indicative of his bewilderment. His closing paragraph betrayed his mood: "What a trouble I am to your excellency in giving you such long details about such paltry affairs? But Sir tho they are paltry yet these very things for want of proper management do very great injury and I am fixed while I remain here and things continue in their present Deplorable State not to fail talking about these evils. Evils that require no great skill of address at least to mend. To keep things in such a situation when they may be mended is conduct too strange to talk about. I do all I can do. I will do since I am in the business. But should I servive this campaign and preserve my reputation I shall count myself a Fortunate Man Indeed. I shall cease saying more upon this subject for the present. But I am truly sick of it."

He continued to work night and day to cope with these marauding parties. If the Tories and Indians would only come in a large group he could collect all his troops and meet them in battle. These sly attacks on isolated settlements were like stabs in the back. The settlers were killed and scalped before they knew what had happened to them. And Willett usually found out about the raids when it was too late to accomplish anything, but he struggled on, riding up and down the Valley, visiting the twenty forts under his command.

One day, while returning with a scouting party from Fort Herkimer, he stopped at the home of Nicholas Herkimer. The house was occupied by Capt. George Herkimer, a brother of the deceased general. George and his men were laboring in the fields when the colonel and his scouts rode up. Mrs. Herkimer asked if she should call her husband. Without waiting for Willett's reply she stepped up on a seat on the stoop to blow an alarm for her husband.

Willett, seeing the danger of her position, shouted, "Woman, for God's sake, come in or you'll be shot." He seized her by the skirt and hustled her into the house. A bullet entered the post near where she had been standing. If she had remained there a few seconds longer she would have been killed. George Herkimer, hearing the rifle speak, rushed up from the fields. He joined Willett's party in driving off the Indians.

If these dangers in the field had been Willett's only difficulties he might have been less irritable during the early days of September, but the promised levies were not arriving and the men who did appear at Fort Plain were mostly homesick bumpkins who insisted upon being on furlough most of the time, with or without permission. Willett was disgusted. "The levies were raised for the defense of the frontier where they might constantly remain and not be running home every few days," he complained to Clinton.

The problem was aggravated by the addition of Capt. Abraham Livingston and several officers from Albany who were fond of playing cards far into the night, not only disturbing the colonel's repose but also upsetting the entire garrison. The group tried the patience of the commandant once too often. They congregated in the officers' quarters and entered into a card game which carried on long after midnight. The colonel listened to the racket until his patience became exhausted. He appeared in his doorway in his long nightshirt and hailed the sentinel. The officers were to stop the noise immediately! The racket continued as the sentinel reported back to Willett that the officers "would be damned if they went out." The corporal of the guard was Willett's second messenger. He went to the cardplayers and told them they were disturbing the colonel's slumbers. He returned with the reply that they were in their own quarters. Why didn't the colonel go down the hill and sleep under a stack of hay?

By this time Willett was thoroughly aroused. He called the officer of the day. That officer was to go to the officers, order the owner of the room confined and send the other officers to their quarters. And have the lights put out, by all means. This was frontier fort. It wasn't a gay city in time of peace. The officer failed to return.

Willett climbed into his trousers and stalked out to see for himself. He found his last messenger arguing with the officers. Livingston was saying sarcastically that "he would go to the colonel and fall on his knees and beg him to let him stay in his quarters, for he had no other."

The tall colonel stared him down. Turning on his heel he left the room, taking the officer of the day with him.

The offenders were arrested and placed in the guardhouse, where they languished until Willett had time for a Court of Inquiry, which found them guilty of disturbing the peace, insulting the colonel and refusing to obey his orders. Except for one brief spell, when they left quarters without permission, the four officers were in confinement all fall.

Major Villafranche was in charge at Fort Herkimer, where

he was dealing out the stores removed from Fort Stanwix. He also was repairing the fortifications. Batteaux laden with ammunition came down the river frequently, to be returned with provisions for the German Flatts. Villafranche visited Fort Plain occasionally. He was an experienced engineer who had been sent to the Valley to improve the forts. He agreed with Willett that the top-heavy blockhouse might topple off the hill. It also might fail to stop a cannonball. The two officers, in a moment of deviltry, decided to put the blockhouse to the test. They had the artillerymen haul out a six-pounder and aim it at the tall guardian of the northern slope. A crowd gathered to see the show. A puff of smoke, a roar which reverberated against the hills and cannonball embedded itself in the hillside. It had gone completely through the blockhouse. Laughter convulsed the gathering, but not for long, for a moment's reflection brought home to the spectators the realization that the fortification which had been under construction for a year was useless against an artillery attack. There was only one thing to do. Villafranche would have to come down with his artificers and rebuild the blockhouse.

It could not be done now. The soldiers were all out protecting the harvest. And rumors of the approach of Walter Butler filled the Valley. Tragedy came quickly to Fort Dayton. Capt. Solomon Woodworth with a party of 39 men and two officers was ambushed on the banks of the West Canada Creek. Only 15 men returned to tell the story. They came bearing the body of their leader and sent back after 11 other men who had been killed. Willett, riding up furiously from Fort Plain, learned that several men were missing, probably in captivity. A few days before Cobleskill, far to the south, had been attacked. The soldiers at Fort Dubois had been enjoying themselves robbing Tory henroosts. The Tories had bided their time. They had joined with a party of Indians, burned several houses, killed and scalped a boy, and rustled off the cattle, while the few defenders inside the fort had watched, being too weak to take the field against the marauders.

Matters at Fort Plain were coming to a head. The disgruntled officers were still confined to their quarters. The levies were dissatisfied because they had neither suitable clothing for the cold weather nor any promise of remuneration for their services. Willett wrote to Governor Clinton, stating that in his opinion money and clothing were the best means of procuring and keeping soldiers. Land and speculation in land might do something, but the colonel did not understand that business. Clinton replied that Congress had agreed to pay the levies, but they had recommended that the states advance the pay on the credit of the United States, and Clinton had not been able to get the legislature to make provisions for any further outlay at its last session. He also sent news of the victory of the French fleet over the British.

Willett had shot two deserters that day, not a pleasant task. He thanked Clinton for the news, adding: "May it pave the way for our speedy entrance into the long lost Metropolis of this State."

Walter Butler Is Here!

WALTER BUTLER IS HERE!

The news came from Currytown on October 24th. Colonel Willett had just answered a false alarm at Fort Herkimer. He had thought that the danger was over for the present, but it had broken forth, this time with terrific force. A scouting party from Fort Plain was in the vicinity of Sharon Springs. Two of the men asked permission to leave the party to visit relatives in Currytown. They contacted the enemy, who were approaching the Mohawk from the southwest. Running rapidly, they eluded the enemy and spread the alarm. At Willow Basin they encountered a funeral party, which broke up while the men ran to warn neighbors. The two scouts reached the Mohawk, totally exhausted. They were captured, but the news was carried to Fort Plain.

Meanwhile the enemy made for the Mohawk, plundering and killing. They captured several members of the funeral party. Major Ross was in command, with Walter Butler as his assistant. They took the new road over Stone Ridge, continued through Auriesville and Florida, forded the Schoharie Creek at its mouth and crossed the Mohawk. News arrived at Fort Plain that they were threatening Schenectady.

Here was the chance for which Willett had longed. This was no raid by scattered groups; it was a mass invasion of the Mohawk Valley. He had promised Washington that if the enemy came in force he would attack them and force them to fight. By the night of the 25th his hastily-gathered force had reached Fort Hunter at the mouth of Schoharie Creek. The Mohawk was scarcely passable at that place, but news had arrived that the enemy were marching toward Johnstown. It would take too long to go down the river to a better fording place. The river was crossed with difficulty. Men floundered in the deep, cold water. Animals slipped on the rocky bottom. Several cases of ammunition toppled into the water, thus diminishing a supply which was scanty at best. But the brave little army of levies and militia hurried on. What the men lacked in discipline, they made up for in enthusiasm. These men were defending their homes. The large party for which they had waited had arrived at last. Hadn't "The Devil" told them that if they could once force the enemy into a pitched battle their troubles would be over? Ross and his men had been moving for days. They must be tired. They would undoubtedly halt at Johnstown for the night. If the pursuers could catch up with them, the British would have to give battle. The contest would be crucial. Either the Mohawk Valley would have to submit to the dominance of Tories or it would be freed of their interference forever.

Silently, doggedly, the little band climbed the hills which rolled up from the river. Colonel Rowley had joined forces with Willett; his Massachusetts men were experienced fighters. Dawn brought them to the outskirts of the colony which Sir William Johnson had founded in the wilderness. Sure enough, the enemy were encamped near his palatial residence.

Colonel Willett had 416 men. Ross' party consisted of 700 British regulars, Tories and Indians. The enemy strength had been forced from the lips of a British regular who had been captured. Both sides were fatigued by forced marches. Again Willett had to resort to strategy to gain his end. He divided his force, sending Rowley to make a circuit through the woods in order to reach the rear of the enemy. The right wing, commanded by Willett himself, moved out onto the field occupied by Ross' forces. The militia and levies, charged by Willett's own enthusiasm, advanced rapidly, exchanging shots with the defenders, who began a retreat toward the woods, a movement which would throw them at the mercy of Rowley. All was going well. Victory, complete victory, would soon be in the hands of the Americans.

The fighting was bitter, often hand to hand. Tomahawks, bayonets, clubs, even fists were used by men whose hatred of each other had been fanned by years of warfare. The air rang with cries of pain and triumph, the scalp yells of the Indians sounding clearly over the more guttural calls of the German militiamen. Slowly but certainly the enemy were being driven back.

Something unaccountable happened. A militiaman, struck by the horror of it all, turned tail and ran. His neighbors, catching the infection, joined him. Soon Willett's force was running headlong toward the village. The colonel rode among them, shouting, imploring, even striking at them with his sword. It was all to no avail. An uncontrollable panic had struck the inexperienced farmers. There was no stopping it. In their haste to leave the field, the artillerymen abandoned the only field piece Willett possessed. It was headlong, disgraceful rout.

Colonel Willett's heart almost stopped beating. It was useless for him to ride back and forth among those stampeded cattle, so he galloped to the village, where he took up his post near the church. Here he and his officers intercepted the panting men, corralled them and prepared to save the force from surrender.

A steady fire rose from the left. Rowley was advancing with his 60 Massachusetts troops and a company of militia. Darkness was falling over the bloody field as the brave little detachment moved forward. Willett, realizing that Rowley would be overwhelmed, rallied his frightened militia and levies and advanced toward Johnson Hall. Another bloody battle seemed about to begin.

The British, tired and discouraged, stood off the two advancing bodies for a few moments and then retired six miles into the woods, leaving Willett in complete possession of the field.

The American force, tired but triumphant, scoured the adjacent woods for dead, wounded and trophies of war. Forty of them had been killed in the battle; many more were wounded, some of them critically. Enemy wounded were groaning in the woods. By torchlight, Willett rounded them up. He took 50 prisoners in all.

The exhausted Americans had lost their fight. It was useless for Willett to pursue the enemy. It would be better to go back to the Valley, gather more troops and try to intercept Ross before he could reach his boats on Oneida Lake. So Willett rode to Fort Dayton, his little army following in rather bedraggled condition.

Fifty Oneida Indians appeared at Fort Dayton, willing and anxious to join in the pursuit. Willett picked his party carefully, choosing only those men who were in good physical condition and who were accustomed to wilderness warfare. News had filtered in to Fort Dayton that the enemy had given up all idea of returning to their boats and were proceeding through the wilderness toward either Buck's Island or Oswego. If they were to be captured, the pursuing force must move swiftly to intercept them.

Willett started from Fort Dayton with about 500 picked men and the 50 Oneidas. The weather was cold. A soft snow was falling. The West Canada Creek had to be forded. The men took off their woollen pantaloons and waded through the frigid waters. They jumped up and down on the other shore and ran to bring back circulation before donning their garments. Snow continued to fall, blowing directly into the faces of the men who were climbing the heights above the creek. At dusk the army camped in a thick wood in the Jerseyfield country. As far as the eye could reach stretched miles and miles of virgin timber, dotted with lakes and lined with streams.

Willett wanted to locate the enemy. At dawn he offered to relieve from duty any man who would shinny up a tall tree that he pointed out. A militiaman threw off his coat, climbed the tree and reported a light a short distance to the northeast. Willett consulted his compass. The Jerseyfield road, near which he was encamped and the old trail to the Mount clearing came together a short distance this side of Black Creek. The light indicated that the British were encamped within the triangle, probably near the Mount trail. Three scouts were sent out. Two came back to report that Ross was encamped there and had no sentries out. One scout remained to observe his movements.

Breakfast was a hurried affair. Willett wanted to get going, for he figured that, by a forced march, he could intercept the British party where the two trails met. The Jerseyfield road wasn't much more than a path through the wilderness. The men slipped and stumbled on roots that projected through the layer of snow. They reached the junction to find that the enemy had already passed that way. The solitary scout, an artilleryman, lay dead beside the road.

Indians appeared ahead, then some Tories. The Americans skirmished with them, capturing some and killing others. From the prisoners Willett learned that this rear guard had been detailed to pick up what provision they could and to follow. Ross' men were tired and in dire need of food.

The Americans came up with the main body of the enemy, who fired a few shots and trotted down the path toward the West Canada Creek. Scouts told Willett that there was a fording place ahead. If he could catch the enemy before they reached the shallow water, there would be no avenue of escape for the British. Willett spurred his men forward.

The West Canada appeared through an opening in the trees, amber, snake-like, its surface dotted with snow-capped stones. At that moment the clouds lifted and the sun came through, revealing the opposite shore. Indians lurked in the woods; the occasional flash of a red or a green coat could be seen behind trees. The whole body of the enemy had succeeded in fording the stream.

A short distance downstream an officer was kneeling beside the swift waters; he was dipping his cup as if to take a drink. He raised his head and glared defiantly at his pursuers.

Willett stiffened. There was no doubt in his mind as to the identity of this officer. Willett had seen that sullen, sneering face during the court martial at the German Flatts. He had heard it described by the terror-stricken inhabitants of the Valley. If Walter Butler could be captured, the whole Valley would be restored to confidence. Willett hurried forward.

A shot rang out behind him. The British officer clutched at his hat, a silly grin spreading over his swarthy face. He remained kneeling, his head inclining toward one shoulder. The scalp-yell rang against the woods. An Oneida was dancing across the stones. He rushed toward the helpless officer, who raised his hand pleadingly. The tomahawk gleamed for a split second and descended. Walter Butler lay on the ground, his blood darkening the white sands along the West Canada.

When Willett reached the other shore, Butler lay face down, the gold braid of his hat mingling with the sand. The Oneida bent over him, begging Willett's permission to lift the scalp.

Willett often had prevented Oneidas from taking scalps. He abhorred the practice. But this was an exception. Turning to the Oneida chief who stood beside him he said, "He belongs to your party, Colonel Lewis." He plunged into the woods in pursuit of the enemy, who were trotting along in Indian file. The Americans chased the British for six miles without catching up with them. Night was coming on. The way ahead was a tangled wilderness. With provisions low and Fort Dayton a long way behind, it was useless and dangerous to continue the pursuit, so Willett gathered his men and reforded the West Canada.

The Indians were making merry. The possessor of Butler's scalp was waving it in the face of a captured British officer. The Oneida was dressed in Butler's coat. Willett asked to examine it. In the pocket he found the same commission that Butler had presented during the trial at the German Flatts. Willett slipped it into his own pocket.

On the opposite shore Walter Butler lay naked, he having been stripped of his clothing by the Indians. His body was never buried.

The tired army started for Fort Dayton, carrying with them a little girl whom the enemy had released in their headlong flight. The artilleryman-scout had been the only American casualty. His body was placed under the roots of a tree that had been felled by the wind. Several axemen proceeded to cut off the trunk. The roots were pushed back over the cavity, effectually protecting the dead soldier from marauding beasts.

The people at Fort Dayton greeted Willett and his men as conquering heroes. A feast was spread on tables near the fort and the whole community made merry. It was a glorious day for the German Flatts. Hadn't Walter Butler been killed? Hadn't news just come up the Valley that Lord Cornwallis had surrendered at Yorktown? The war, the long, weary war, would soon be over.

Colonel Marinus Willett returned to Fort Plain, where he reported the campaign in detail to Governor Clinton, closing with these words: "In this situation to the compassion of a Starving Wilderness we left them. In a fair way of receiving a punishment better suited to their merits than a musquet Ball a Tomahawk or Captivity."

His Regimental Orders for November 2, 1781 told the story of the campaign in a nutshell: "We pursued them as closely and warmly as possible nor did they ever attempt to check us in our advance except at one difficult ford in Canada Crick where they lost several of their men amongst their killed at this place was Walter Butler, the person who commanded the Massacre at Cherry Valley in 1778. He was called a Major But By the Commission found in his pocket appears to be no more than a Captain . . . Their flight was performed in an Indian file upon a constant trot and one man being knocked in the head or falling off into the woods never stopped the progress of his neighbour. Nor even the fall of their favoright Butler could attract their attention so much as to Induce them to take even the money or any thing out of his Pocket altho he was not dead when found by one of our Indians, who finished his business for him and got a Considerable booty."

Failure at Oswego

SECURITY HAD COME to the Mohawk Valley. Occasional raids carried on by small bands of Indians were often beaten off without loss of life or property. Families were returning to their holdings, carrying the few pitiful possessions that they had been able to take with them in their flight. Hadn't rumors of peace been circulated? Premature, perhaps, but nevertheless satisfying to people who were anxious to grasp any straw of hope. So back they came, the courageous ones. The woods rang with the stroke of the axe once more.

Marinus Willett was satisfied with his regiment. Recruiting had been more successful, now that the state legislature had offered bounties of money rather than land. Four hundred well-trained troops were garrisoning the forts from Schenectady to the German Flatts. The autumn had been occupied in building new barracks at Fort Plain and other forts. Willett had taken the precaution of having all those soldiers inoculated who had not undergone the terrors of smallpox. His own quarters were roomy and comfortable. All that was needed was Mary, who had been lonely since the death of Young Marinus. The colonel, busy on the frontier, had little time to be lonely but Mary, living away from her home and husband, was feeling the strain. Toward the end of November Willett rode down the Valley in excellent spirits. His military career had been a success, even though he had not been with the Grand Army. The papers had been enthusiastic in their praise. He had gained the freedom of the city of Albany. And, better than anything else, he had won the unqualified approval of his hero, George Washington. What more could a man ask?

After imparting the news to Mary that he had fitted up comfortable quarters for her at Fort Plain, he rowed across the Hudson to visit Washington, who was in camp at Newburgh. He was greeted with that friendliness which His Excellency always bestowed upon his favorite officers. Would he stay to dinner?

They ate together, hero and hero-worshipper. It was a pleasant meal. Washington had much to learn about the frontier and Willett was full of information. At the close the colonel rose to leave. Washington asked him into his office. Questions were asked pertaining to the success of Willett's recruiting and to the strength and situation of the men in the colonel's regiment. Willett, knowing that all was in excellent condition along the Mohawk, spoke enthusiastically about prospects in that section. With peace about to be declared, he had decided to bring Mrs. Willett to Fort Plain, where a quiet winter was expected.

Washington interrupted him. Now he was His Excellency, the Commander-in-Chief of the Continental Army. He informed Willett that little reliance would be placed upon immediate peace. The British were still strong in certain places. Their troops were occupying New York City. Canada had not been subdued. Fort Oswego constituted a menace to the northern frontier, for most of the raiding parties gathered at that place. Washington came to the point. Was Willett acquainted with the strength of the enemy garrison at Fort Oswego? Willett was. Did he think the fort could be surprised and taken by an expedition in mid-winter?

Willett saw the handwriting on the wall. Visions of a pleasant winter in company of his wife began to fade. Washington did not press him for an answer. Would Willett think over the possibilities of an attack on Oswego and write his opinion?

Willett was back at Fort Plain a week later without Mary. For the first time in his life he was not anxious to attain military glory. Yet he could not refuse his hero, nor could he ignore his duty to his country. He wrote to Washington, giving his favorable opinion of the possibilities of an attack on Oswego.

Washington, knowing that Willett would concur, was already in motion. He wrote Willett from Newburgh on December 18, informing him that the clothier at headquarters could furnish vests, woollen hose, woollen caps, socks and mittens sufficient for the whole party. Willett would have to procure the necessary Indian moccasins and snowshoes. Washington did not see why each man should have a pair of the latter. He also recommended that axes, saws, augers and a gouge should be taken along, so that scaling ladders could be made when the party reached a position near the fort. Would Willett pick his guides carefully, for the persons who were to precede the main party must necessarily be men of tried fidelity? The failure of a guide might result in defeating the whole purpose of the expedition, which was to take Fort Oswego by surprise.

Willett planned the campaign with his usual attention to detail. The time was chosen with care. On the morning of the 10th of February the moon would set late. There would be an excellent opportunity to fall upon Oswego in that interval between moonset and sunrise. Willett sent his plan to Washington, who approved it and added that he would appear personally at Fort Herkimer to see the expedition off if sleighing should be good enough at the time. Willett would please tell no one of his coming. The colonel could act on his own judgment regarding the rendezvous at Fort Herkimer, for he knew the situation better than anyone else. One hundred and fifty blankets, all that were in the clothier's store at Newburgh, were being sent to Albany on Feb. 2, along with 25 axes. It was not possible to send medicine and bandages because of lack of time to procure them. Would Willett send to Albany for the blankets and axes? Horses and sleighs would be required to accompany the troops. Washington wrote Willett, authorizing him to "take from the Inhabitants by Impress, if necessary, such a number of Sleighs & Horses as may be requisite to carry into Execution the . . . Expedition against the Enemys Post at Oswego."

The troops assembled at Fort Herkimer on February 8th. Evidently sleighing was bad, for Washington did not come up to see them off. The next morning they marched to Oneida Lake, moving hurriedly along the road past Oriskany and the ruins of Fort Stanwix, sliding down Wood Creek on the ice. After halting at the lake to eat and catch their breaths, the troops plodded on all night across the ice of Oneida Lake. It was a cold, blowy journey, one which taxed the breaths and legs of the troops. Willett had known Oneida Lake in April, when Van Schaick's party had been marooned on an island for a whole day, waiting for the wind to stop blowing. It was blowing now, a cold, icy gale which cut his cheeks and caused him to flail his arms across his chest to keep up circulation. The men marched in a long queue, blowing on their hands, rushing into double-quick now and then to keep from freezing. By two o'clock the next afternoon the party was at Oswego Falls, thirteen miles from its destination.

A camp was set up and the men ate the cooked provisions they had brought with them. Any fire might be detected by lurking Indians and thus defeat the purpose of the expedition. Men were sent into the woods with axes and saws. They hauled into camp slender trunks of trees, which were cut up by the carpenters and fashioned into eight crude scaling ladders.

The order to march was given. The woods were deep with snow, but the river wound ahead, bare where the high wind had blown the white masses away. The party took to the river, sliding and slipping along until they were within four miles of Oswego. Here Willett halted them and called to him Captain John and two other Indians. The colonel had known Captain John for years. He placed complete confidence in this Oneida. It was ten o'clock and the moon was riding the sky. In four hours the time would be ripe for the surprise attack. All plans had been arranged. Each officer knew his assignment. The river ice here was weak. Would Captain John and his Oneidas guide them by land to the fort? Captain John nodded. He knew the country backward and forward.

The snow lay deeper here and the cold seeped into the veins of the tired soldiers struggling through the woods. But they plodded on, those without snowshoes sinking almost to their waists in the impeding whiteness. There were no murmurs of complaint, for the men were filled with enthusiasm at the prospect of the booty which would fall to them at Oswego. The two forts were known to be comfortable. It would be pleasant to lie in good bunks that night after a hearty meal from the British larder. There was no hurry about getting back to the Mohawk Valley. That section was safe from Indian attacks. Hadn't they helped Willett to drive away Butler and his Tories? Wasn't the body of that enemy of liberty rotting beside the West Canada Creek?

Two hours passed. No opening in the woods was reached. They all knew that they should be before Oswego, but they were still struggling through the deep snow. The men were having a difficult time with the ladders, which caught in the snow-laden firs and had to be extricated with numb fingers. Willett encouraged the men to greater efforts, but in his mind rankled the thought that something had gone wrong. Four miles? It seemed as if they had gone ten. So he hurried to the front in time to meet a disconsolate group of three. Captain John, completely crestfallen, admitted that he had been following Indian snowshoe tracks, hoping that they would take the party to Oswego. Instead, they had led to an Indian settlement far from the British fort. John and his Indians were lost!

The party halted in a swamp. The men were sinking through the thin ice. Their feet were wet. Some of them complained of pains in their toes and ankles. Discouragement was stamped on their faces by the feeble light of a moon that was slipping behind the firs. The time for the attack had come, but the party was wandering in a trackless wilderness, miles from its objective.

Through Willett's mind flashed the orders of Washington: "If you fail in surprising the fort, the attempt will be unwarrantable." If he failed? Willett had failed, for the first time in his military career. He had failed in his best chance for success. His plans had been well laid. His party was prepared and full of enthusiasm. Only one link in the chain had not been forged. He stared at Captain John, who lowered his eyes. The other Oneidas were disconsolate shadows against the snow. Willett was convinced that the Indians had not intentionally led him astray. The Oneidas had always been partial to the American cause and Captain John was his friend. He gave the order to retreat.

It was a horrible flight. Cold, inexpressable cold, filled the dawn. The snow seemed deeper than before, the ice more insecure. Many men were limping. Two lay down in the snow, silently, without complaint. They became part of the northern forest. The army limped on, men supporting their comrades, even carrying them. Provisions ran out before they reached Oneida Lake. The soldiers, remembering several barking dogs they had shot on the trip north, dug in the snow for their carcasses, cooked and ate them. Oneida Lake was a horrible experience. Gasping and blowing, the men fought for breath; clouds of vapor rose from their opened mouths, froze on their cheeks, eyelashes and forelocks. The relentless wind cut through their hunting shirts and woollen mittens.

Their feet resembled stumps. But they hurried on without complaint. And Colonel Marinus Willett, his heart beating dully beneath his waistcoat of Russian drilling, walked with head bowed. There was nothing he could say.

A letter awaited him at Fort Plain; it was sealed with the stamp of His Excellency. Willett opened it slowly. Washington sincerely hoped the letter would meet Willett "returning successfull" from his expedition.

The colonel grasped a reluctant pen and wrote to Clinton and to Washington. He did not cover up his failure. There were no alibis, only a touch of bitterness at his own confidence in Captain John. The closing paragraph of his letter to Washington revealed his feelings: "I can't help feeling great regret at the disappointment whilst I reflect with gratitude at the honor Confered in me by your Excellency in affording me an opportunity of atchieving so much at so small a risk. I pretend not to say that the work has been performed as well as it might have been done, perhaps I have been deficient in points of discernment. But I am sure I have not been so in points of Integrity & exertions. These have been stretched to the Utmost. Yet I have unfortunately failed. Failed at a time when I looked on the prise Just ready to be received, Which was truly the Case from ten o'clock to one o'clock in the night of the twelvth Instant. With everything ready to make the attack we was just within view of the fort Undisscovered. Whilst every breast was filled with ardor & the most Animated determination. But lost it in this strange & unacountable manner that I have before related." To Clinton he wrote: "This expedition has been an ample tryal of our soldier, and I have found that in every respect, they are a match for the most veteran troops we have." Clinton might not understand, but Willett hoped that Washington would not condemn him for his failure. He waited patiently for a reply from his hero.

It came promptly. Willett opened the letter with confidence touched with apprehension. Washington had written: "I have been favoured with your letter of the 19th of February, announcing the failure of your attempt against Oswego. Unfortunate as the circumstance is, I am happy in the persuasion that no imputation or reflection can justly reach your character; and that you are enabled to derive much consolation from the animated zeal, fortitude, and activity of the officers and soldiers who accompanied you. The failure it seems, must be attributed to some of those unaccountable events which are not within the control of human means; and which, though they often occur in military life, yet require, not only the fortitude of the soldier, but the calm reflection of the philosophy to bear.

"I cannot omit expressing to you the high sense I entertain of your persevering exertions and zeal on this expedition; and beg you to accept my warm thanks on the occasion; and that you will be pleased to communicate my gratitude to the officers and men who acted under your command, for the share they had in that service."

Willett must have read this letter with a feeling of relief. In it Washington revealed all the nobility of his own character. He too had suffered reverses, many of them. He had won out over them all. Marinus Willett too would emerge victorious.

He was to need courage. Whisperings had begun at Fort Plain before Christmas, nasty bits of gossip concerning his intimate relations with Mrs. Seeber. Willett, accustomed to fighting Tories and Indians on the battlefield, was ill-equipped to stand up under a barrage of female tongues. The men understood. That was part of military life on a frontier outpost. Women were different. Willett was glad that Mary had not come to Fort Plain for the winter. Possibly he had been stupid in asking her. She would have been tossed into the midst of this scandal. She would have braved it, Willett had no doubt, but it would have been difficult for her. So the colonel went about his business, tight-lipped, unsmiling.

The child was born, a strapping boy. Willett acknowledged it immediately and it was christened Marinus Willett Seeber. The colonel took the boy under his wing and paid for his education until he arrived at maturity. Young Seeber eventually returned to Fort Plain, set himself up as a dancing master, and tried in vain to win the affections of the townsfolk. The taint was upon him. He lasted but a short time at Fort Plain and what became of him no one seems to know.

Colonel Willett was in Albany in April of 1783 when the news of the signing of the peace treaty was proclaimed by the town clerk from the steps of the city hall. He met the messengers from Philadelphia and dispatched two Indian runners to Saratoga and the lakes, paying them thirty dollars and furnishing them with new shirts and stocks. He also saw off two messengers for the Mohawk Valley; they were to carry the news to the British garrisons at Oswego and Niagara.

Major Andrew Fink, commanding in Willett's absence, delegated Captain Alexander Thompson, an artillery officer, to carry the news from Fort Plain to Major Ross at Oswego. Thompson left the fort with three companions, one of them bearing a white flag attached to a long spear. Willett was at Fort Herkimer when the flag returned. Thompson reported that on his way to Oswego he had met two canoes loaded with Indians and that he had persuaded them to return to Oswego, where he found Major Ross quite agreeable to the cause of peace.

The army organization was kept up until autumn. A party of Indians killed and scalped two men within sight of Fort Plain a few days after Thompson left for Oswego. Then all became quiet.

Willett chafed at his post. When would it be possible for him to go back to New York to settle his affairs? The people were coming back up the Valley, loaded with supplies and furniture, to occupy the new cabins which would spring up like magic from the blackened ruins of their former homes. They passed Fort Plain and Fort Herkimer, plodding courageously toward the rich land drained by the Mohawk west of those frontier outposts. Nothing was to be feared now. "The Devil" had driven the Indians and the Tories out forever.

In July General Washington made a trip of inspection through the Mohawk Valley. He stopped at Fort Plain, where he was entertained by Colonel Clyde and the inhabitants. Willett met him at Fort Herkimer and rode with him toward Oneida Lake. One can imagine the pride with which the lanky colonel told of the the famous siege of Fort Stanwix. The men also talked of Indian fighting. Washington contended that the Virginia method of letting the men scatter from tree to tree and fight Indian fashion was the most effective. Willett, from his experience against the Iroquois, had found that method unsuccessful. He favored charging the Indians and disconcerting them by yelling and huzzaing louder than they did. He finally won Washington's admission that the latter method was probably better suited to the Northern Indians.

This ride along the Mohawk closed Colonel Marinus Willett's military career. It must have been a source of pleasure to him to have completed it at the side of the Commander-in-Chief. After 25 years Willett had caught up with his hero.

III
RETREAT

1783–1812

High Sheriff

THE BRITISH EVACUATED New York City on November 28, 1783. General Washington entered from the north, rode through streets lined with cheering thousands and watched the Stars and Stripes replace the Union Jack at the Battery. A few days later he said farewell to his officers at Fraunces' Tavern and departed for Mount Vernon. Marinus Willett, watching his hero leave, probably realized that a chapter of his own life had been closed.

New York had been under military rule for seven years. The city had been damaged by fire, first in 1776 and again in 1778. Fortifications dotted the landscape at strategic points. Fort George was being used for stabling horses. Houses sorely needed repair. The streets were cluttered with filth. Hogs rooted in the gutters. The population had declined during the war but was being augmented daily by refugees returning from Connecticut and the Hudson Valley. The housing situation had become critical.

Two days after the British evacuation Governor Clinton ordered Colonel Willett and Colonel John Lasher to take possession, care and custody of all forfeited lands and tenements in the city until the legislature could be convened and make provision for selling them. Willett and Lasher were not to take any lands or tenements held by bona fide lease, demise or contract from any person or persons made at any time before the British garrison was withdrawn from the city.

They were to permit lands and tenements to be occupied by persons who had removed from the city in 1776 who appeared to them destitute of habitation, but the agents were to be sure to have these persons sign notes or memoranda in writing, stating that they occupied the tenements out of will to Willett and Lasher, with an agreement to pay rent such as was to be determined by the legislature.

The Council for the Southern District, a temporary government set up as early as 1779, announced two elections. The first, on December 15th, was to choose aldermen and assistant aldermen. The second, on the 29th, was to seat members of the state legislature from the Southern District. The Council broadened the suffrage by cutting in two the financial requirements for voting. This act was a boon to the Sons of Liberty, for though they had been the most enthusiastic leaders of the revolt against Great Britain, few of them had been enfranchised. They ran a ticket which consisted of General John Lamb, Colonel Isaac Sears, Colonel Marinus Willett, Captain Henry Rutgers and other radical Whigs. They campaigned vigorously. Broadsides were issued. Newspaper advertisements and articles appeared regularly. Speeches were made by the candidates to large audiences. Tories were intimidated. The election ran from December 29th to January 5th. The Sons of Liberty took an early lead which they never relinquished. Their whole ticket of nine men was chosen, Marinus Willett receiving the largest number of votes.

Willett did not take his seat in the legislature. George Clinton was seeking a better office for the colonel. He and the Council of Appointment offered Willett the position of High Sheriff of the city and county of New York and the colonel accepted it. The decision was a fortunate one for Willett, for the wave of Tory reaction in the following year unseated Lamb, Rutgers and Sears.

Marinus Willett took the oath of office as High Sheriff on

February 7, 1784 at the inn of John Simmons in Wall Street not far from the City Hall. On the same occasion were sworn in James Duane as Mayor and Richard Varick as Recorder, also the ward aldermen and their assistants.

New York was a disorderly city. Robberies occurred frequently. Citizens were ordered to lock their doors at night to prevent criminals from entering their homes. Willett supervised the hanging of two highwaymen at the gallows in The Fields. The body of a young woman was found floating in the North River. She had been cruelly murdered. Practical jokers had a habit of running through the streets yelling "Fire" without giving the location of the conflagration. Taxes on property were in arrears. Willett spent much of his time conducting sheriff's sales at the Coffee House on Water Street.

He had official functions to attend. Fourth of July was a day of rejoicing, as was the anniversary of the evacuation of the city. Lafayette visited New York and was presented with the freedom of the city in a gold box. He was entertained royally and was escorted by his brother officers to the ship *Nymphe,* in which he departed for France, not to return for 40 years.

The most serious disturbance during Willett's term of four years was the "Doctors' Mob." Medical students at the hospital on Broadway, desiring cadavers upon which to practice, had been rifling the graves in potter's field and the Negro burying ground. Rumors flew fast. The hospital became an object of horror to a certain group in the city. The students became tactless. One afternoon in the winter of 1787-1788 some youngsters were playing in the rear of the hospital. A young surgeon, thinking to have some fun, held up an amputated arm. One boy became curious and climbed to the top of a fence to get a closer view of the specimen. The surgeon told the youngster that he was looking at his own mother's arm. The boy turned pale. He slid down from the fence and ran away as fast as his legs would carry him. The doctor, laughing, went back into the hospital.

The storm broke toward evening. It seems that the boy had lost his mother recently. Frightened and horrified at the surgeon's words, he had run to his father, a mason working on Broadway. The parent and the boy had hurried to potter's field, where the mother had been buried. They had found the grave empty!

Marinus Willett got a summons from Mayor Duane to hasten to the hospital. He arrived to find that a mob had ransacked the hospital and had destroyed valuable medical instruments. It was threatening the lives of the doctors. Willett took the medical students into custody and the crowd quieted down.

They re-assembled the following morning. The Mayor and the High Sheriff rode up Broadway in imposing procession. They spoke of conciliation to the crowd, but their words fell upon barren ground. They departed after promising an investigation. The crowd lingered, to be joined by hundreds of artisans and laborers. They marched in a solid body to The Fields, where the doctors and medical students had been placed in the jail. Cries of "Bring out your doctors!" rang through the air. Hamilton and John Jay harangued the mob, but they were driven to retirement under a barrage of bricks and stones.

The Mayor was still for conciliation but Willett talked him into calling a small body of militia. The crowd parted and let the militia through but did not retreat. An impasse had been reached. A detail of a dozen mlitiamen were marching up Broadway. The crowd rushed them, snatched the muskets from their shoulders and broke them on the ground. "To the jail!" rang the cry. The mob stormed the barricaded doors and windows but were driven back.

Dusk was falling when the measured tread of a large body of militia sounded on Broadway. The mob, thoroughly aroused and inspired by success, derided the militia and met their advance with a shower of stones.

Baron von Steuben had joined the authorities. He pleaded with Mayor Duane not to permit the militia to fire on the people. A stone caught him in the head and knocked him down. While lying on the ground he yelled, "Fire, Mayor, Fire!"

The order came, "Ready—aim—fire!"

Several men toppled to the ground. Others clutched at their sides, reeling. The seriousness of the situation dawned on the mob, which broke and fled in all directions. At the cost of several lives the "Doctors' Mob" had been repulsed, but the jail was guarded by the militia for several days, while deep resentment filled the city.

Governor Clinton also had need for Willett's services. Up in Massachusetts the conservatives had defeated the populists and had refused relief to impoverished veterans of the war. The hill farmers felt the full weight of the blow, for farms were taxed five shillings an acre regardless of value and the poll tax was shared equally regardless of wealth. The change in the value of currency threatened them with ruin. One Daniel Shays rose as a leader of a rabble army in the western part of the state. He closed the court at Worcester and forced the court in Springfield to adjourn. General Benjamin Lincoln marched with his militia in the dead of winter, through night and a blizzard, to defeat Shays at Petersham. The rebels fled in all directions, many of them seeking refuge in New York, where they continued to agitate against the conservatives. The Governor of Massachusetts asked Clinton to refuse admission to the rebels. Clinton, a radical at heart, delayed action, but his hand was forced.

In March, 1787 the New York legislature passed some private resolutions. Clinton, accompanied by Willett and other officials, set out for the northern part of the state. They met General Lincoln at New Lebanon and rode with him to

Pittsfield. All was quiet. Shays and other leaders were reported to be at St. John's en route to Canada. They were later apprehended and punished. Clinton and his party returned to New York, satisfied that they had made a step toward cooperation between the states.

The wave of conservatism which had downed Shays in Massachusetts was also sweeping New York. With the re-enfranchisement of Loyalists, New York City returned to its status as a stronghold of merchants and propertied men. Alexander Hamilton, who had defended Loyalist claims brilliantly in the courts, rose as the leader of the conservative element. John Jay and Governeur Morris also were active in this reaction. The Constitutional Convention met and drew up a document which received the condemnation of the Clintonians and the Sons of Liberty. George Clinton, who had been supreme in the state for ten years, was unwilling to relinquish any of his power to a national government. The Sons of Liberty were reaping the reward of their labors. They refused to make any concessions to the group which surrounded Hamilton. Marinus Willett, being both a Clintonian and a Son of Liberty, joined in the opposition to Hamilton's ideas.

The election of delegates to the New York convention for ratifying the new Constitution was held in late April, 1788. Among the Clintonian candidates were Aaron Burr and Marinus Willett, who resigned as High Sheriff. They were opposed by Hamilton, Jay and other prominent conservatives. The election was bitterly fought and the Clintonians were badly defeated. A determined minority, led by Melancthon Smith, went to Poughkeepsie to fight Hamilton's plans for nationalization. Young De Witt Clinton, the nephew of the Governor, sat in on all of the sessions and reported to Captain Charles Tillinghast in New York "a regularly account of the proceedings here by as particular and accurate as a week memory will allow."

Smith put up a sterling battle. Outnumbered, deserted by

some of his supporters, the New York lawyer made speeches which vied with those of Hamilton for excellency. During the hot month of July he thundered his arguments against the Constitution, his chief pleas being for an inclusion of a Bill of Rights and other amendments before the document was ratified. His efforts were to no avail. The weight of national opinion overwhelmed him. Eight states had already ratified the Constitution when the New York convention met. The delegates were still arguing as the ratification by the ninth and tenth states reach New York. A grand procession wound its way to The Fields, where two bullocks and six mutton were roasted whole, together with hams and other foods. At the corner of Wall Street and Broadway, encircled by a ring over two feet in diameter, were thirteen stars, ten brilliant, one (New York) half-illuminated, and two (North Carolina and Rhode Island) almost obscure. And on the 26th of July at nine o'clock in the evening a courier arrived from Poughkeepsie with the news that the New York delegates had ratified the Constitution. Bells rang. A salute boomed from the fort. Citizens went to the houses of the members of the convention and cheered.

The enthusiasm of the victors knew no bounds. They remembered that the opposition to the Constitution had been led by Thomas Greenleaf's newspaper. The mob rushed to the editor's home in Pine Street. Greenleaf, who was visiting with friends across the street, heard the roar of their approach. He hurried to his print shop, dismissed his assistants with the exception of one apprentice who refused to go, and prepared to defend his property at the point of a pistol. It was midnight. Greenleaf threw open a window and defied the mob. He was saluted with a shower of stones. Calmly, the editor took aim and blew the fingers off the hand of a sailor in the front ranks. Major Livingston was using an axe on Greenleaf's door. The editor reached an arm out of the window, brought the pistol to within a few feet of Livingston's ear and pulled the trigger. The pistol failed to discharge, but the click drove Livingston away from the door. Greenleaf tried again, but with no result. He and his apprentice fled through a rear door while the attackers ransacked the printshop. The newspaper was discontinued for several days while Greenleaf and his assistants collected their materials from the street.

General John Lamb was also threatened. Tillinghast, his son-in-law, was in Lamb's house on Wall Street when the mob approached. The old warrior sent him home to protect his own family and proceeded to plan the defense of his dwelling. The women were sent to the attic, armed with porter bottles. All doors and windows were barred. The hall was barricaded with furniture. Lamb's little army of three veterans of the Revolution, two seventeen-year-olds and a Negro servant stood at the head of the stairs; the boys and the Negro were prepared to reload the pistols fired by their elders.

The crowd gathered below in the moonlight, threatening the general with taunts, abuse and stones. No reply came from within the darkened house, which rose ominously in the green light. The mob leaders held a council of war and decided not to try their strength against Lamb. If an editor could shoot accurately enough to maim one of their leaders, what might a general do? They dispersed, trailing behind them feeble taunts.

The Clintonians refused to accept their defeat gracefully. The Sons of Liberty were also reluctant to relinquish their hard-earned power. Their ranks had been sadly depleted. McDougall, after shifting his affections to the moderate Whigs, had died in 1786. Sears, defeated at the polls in 1784, had sailed for China on a business venture and had been buried there. Of the original radicals only Lamb and Willett remained. They found able assistants in Charles Tillinghast and Melancthon Smith. In October ten radicals met at

Fraunces' Tavern and after some deliberation formed themselves into a society "for the purpose of procuring a general convention of this state." Their design was to undo certain features of the Constitution and to insist upon the inclusion of a Bill of Rights. Marinus Willett was elected chairman and Charles Tillinghast secretary. A motion was proposed by Smith and seconded by Lamb for a committee of three to open correspondence with other states for the purpose of explaining the reasons for the adoption of the Constitution by New York and to ask their assistance in securing the required amendments.

Melancthon Smith published "An Address to the People of the State of New York," explaining his position. He had wished the New York convention to amend the Constitution first and then adopt it. In brief, his objections were:

1. The Constitution would supplant and overturn state governments.
2. The representation in the general legislature was too small to secure liberty for the state.
3. The legislature would have unlimited power of taxation both in respect to direct and indirect taxes.
4. Judicial power could be extended to cases which ought to be reserved to the state courts.
5. The power of the general legislature would include the regulation of the time, place and manner of holding elections.
6. The general legislature would have the power to maintain a standing army without restriction.

Letters were sent to other states. The Sons of Liberty were stubborn, but the time had passed when they could influence the trend toward nationalism. When the first Congress met in New York it stole the thunder from the Sons of Liberty by including in the first ten amendments most of the items which the radicals desired.

George Clinton staggered under the blow, but he managed to be re-elected Governor by the narrow margin of 429 votes, chiefly due to his strength in the upper counties. Willett had served on the committee of correspondence which prepared a circular letter and address to these counties. He also had campaigned vigorously. Clinton did the best he could for his friend. He appointed Willett and four others as assistant justices "for the express purpose of trying causes within the city and county of New York to the value of ten pounds and under."

Evidently this office offered insufficient remuneration for Willett's expenses, for he opened a commission store at 36 Water Street in October "for the reception of GOODS to be disposed of on commission, at Public or Private SALE. Money advanced, previous to sale is required. The excellency of the situation, and his extensive acquaintance with country merchants and traders, induces him to flatter himself that his sales will be advantageous to those who please to favor him with their commands." As a special inducement he offered for sale quantities of Antigua, St. Croix, Barbados and New York rum.

The electors had chosen the first President of the United States. George Washington had received all 60 votes. John Adams would be the first Vice President, he having been given 34 votes. On April 23, 1789 Adams arrived at the state line, where he was met by the militia and officers of distinction. The papers were carrying announcements of the reception to be given Washington, who had passed through Philadelphia that same day. The President was received in New York with pomp. On April 30th the national hero advanced to the front of the balcony of City Hall, laid his hand on his heart, bowed several times and retired to an arm chair, overcome with emotion. He rose again when Chancellor Livingston read the oath of office. He rested his hand upon The Bible. The Secretary of the Senate raised The Book to Washington's lips. A flag was unfurled on the cupola of the City Hall, a signal for the discharge of artillery at the Battery. The destiny of a nation was in the hands of the man who had been most instrumental in winning its freedom.

It was a glorious day for the Republic, but a sad one for the Sons of Liberty. The appointments in New York were being controlled by Alexander Hamilton, who had received the office of Secretary of the Treasury. The only radical to secure a post was John Lamb, who was made Collector of Customs for the Port of New York, a position which kept him in continual hot water. Marinus Willett, who had applied for a position as Marshal, was overlooked, as were most of Clinton's supporters. The colonel evidently decided to remain in the commission business, for he was advertising Jamaica Pimento by the bag, of the best quality, that October.

Substantial Citizen

MARINUS WILLETT HAD PROFITED by the Revolution and the years of Clintonian control. The colonel, shrewd in business matters, had seen the value of the fertile land in the central part of the state and had applied early for bounties. In 1783 he had purchased a tract of 4000 acres at French Catherine's on Seneca Lake, 1000 for himself, 3000 for friends. He also owned, together with Washington and George Clinton, part of the Coxe Patent which lay in the section now stretching from Rome through Westmoreland and New Hartford toward Bridgewater. In 1784 he had bought 700 acres at Hampton Village and a tract of 2000 acres in the northern part of the Steuben Patent near the Ava town line. This latter grant was known as Willett's Patent. To this he added 1500 acres in the town of Ava, known as Willett's Small Patent. He and Melancthon Smith entered petitions for land in Chenango County and, after considerable dickering over prices which varied from two to three shillings an acre, Willett purchased 6000 acres in the Twenty Township for £ 200.

The Loyalists in New York City had departed, leaving valuable property behind them, not only in the city but in Westchester and on Long Island. The Treaty of 1783 restored property and civil privileges to Loyalists who had not borne arms against the new Republic. Combatant Tories were given one year in which to return to their estates. If their lands had been sold in the meantime, they had the right to recover them by refunding the purchase price to the new owner. There was to be no further confiscation. The moderate Whigs wished to act in accordance with the treaty, but New York contained many radicals. Popular sentiment there secured fresh confiscatory measures in disregard to the rulings of the treaty. On May 12, 1784 the New York legislature authorized a speedy sale of confiscated lands. Clinton appointed Isaac Stoutenbergh and Philip Van Cortlandt as Commissioners of Forfeitures for the Southern District. They were to sell "for gold and silver only" Tory property in New York City to the value of £ 20,000. Purchasers were to pay one third of the price on the date of sale and the remainder before June 1, 1785.

Possibly the wealthiest family of Loyalists was that headed by James De Lancey, who had been a stout adherent to the King's cause during the Revolution. His entire estate was confiscated. The East Farm, lying along the East River, was considered particularly desirable. The Livingstons were buying heavily there, as were Nicholas Fish and Morgan Lewis. Marinus Willett and John Lamb did not have much money. Lamb, a wine merchant, had spent much of the war in the field and his business had suffered. William Goforth, by establishing himself in Philadelphia, had saved some of Willett's funds. Yet the two Sons of Liberty wanted to take a hand in this grab of Tory property. The price was ridiculously low. New York would grow. The city might even spread as far as Corlear's Hook, where the De Lancey country seat stood. Willett was willing to take the chance. He and Lamb bought tract three of the East Farm, a large block of land fronting on the East River at Corlear's Hook. They paid £ 96 for it.

Willett did not stop here. He bought lots 1446-51 in the same area. He secured James Jauncey's house and lot in the East Ward for £ 1200 and a part of Henry White's estate for £ 225. And over on Long Island he annexed the 200 acres of Johannes Polhemus, a convicted Tory, for £ 1650.

Much of the De Lancey land was purchased on a speculative basis. The Livingstons, in particular, saw the value of buying property and holding it for later sale. Some of their land was not sold until 1840, the Livingston heirs reaping a fabulous profit from the sales. The outstanding example of clever speculation was the Robert Morris estate on Harlem Heights. This tract of 115 acres containing a large mansion was sold in 1784 for £ 2250. In 1799 Leonard Parkinson got it for $13,000. He sold off most of the land for $27,000 and the remainder to Stephen Jumel, together with the mansion, for about $20,000, realizing a profit of $34,000 on his venture.

Marinus Willett kept his land. In his mind lay the vision of a great mansion on Corlear's Hook, surrounded by well-developed streets whose lots could be sold at a profit. Mary, after wandering around from Danbury to New Windsor for seven years, was entitled to a house equal to any in the city. Willett built for Mary Pearsee the spreading mansion known as Cedar Grove.

The Willett home was a large, two-storey structure with wings snuggled against each end. The central doorway was attractive, and chimneys at the extremes of the roof bespoke of fireplaces beneath them. The house stood in an isolated spot, separated from the city by rolling fields. A picket fence added attractiveness to the expanse of lawn leading to the front door. Gardens were laid out behind the house, also carriageways and arbors. A row of young poplars was set along the fringe of the garden and a small orchard of fruit trees was planted by the colonel. It must have been a happy day for Marinus and Mary Willett when they moved into Cedar Grove. Yet there may have been a touch of sadness, too, for the boy they had lost. Cedar Grove was to remain childless for over a decade.

The radical of 1775 had become the substantial citizen

of 1789. He was the owner of a business house and controlled valuable property, both in the city and the state. After remaining aloof from Trinity Church, he returned to the fold when that institution decided to strike out the names of the King and the royal family from its prayers. Edward Willett, a man nearly 90 years old, forgave his son for his participation in the "rebellion" and came to finish out his days at Cedar Grove.

The old man was fond of recounting a story which his son also used in his later life. Edward Willett, the ardent Loyalist, had told his son before the war that the British would conquer and Marinus would be hanged. The day Marinus left to go with Montgomery in 1775, Edward Willett had said, "My son, I never expect to see you again, for you will either be killed in battle or hung."

At the close of the war Marinus had visited his father in Jamaica and had said, "Well, father, here I am, neither killed nor hung."

The old man had thought for a moment before replying, "I'll tell you, my son. When I was a young man Governor Clinton invited me to dinner, a high honor in those days. Not accustomed to meet such great folks, I determined to do at table just as they did to avoid disgracing myself. After dinner, with the dessert, olives were on the table, which although I had read of in The Bible, I had never seen before. Everybody was praising them, so I took one also. It tasted so nauseous that I could not eat it. I put my hand to my mouth, took the olive out and slyly disposed of it in my pocket. So it is, Marinus, with your independence. What I can't swallow, I must pocket."

Willett's status as a retired officer also brought him into contact with the aristocratic element in the city. Shortly before the close of the war the Society of the Cincinnati had been formed at Newburgh. Its purpose was to continue and strengthen the ties of friendship that had grown up during long service in the War of the Revolution and as far as possible to perpetuate them among its members and their descendants who might be in need, and in some degree to help in maintaining the Union of the States. Requirements for membership, which was limited to officers, were three years in the army or active participation at the close of the war. The eldest male descendants of officers who had died in the service were also eligible. The original members contributed one month's pay to the society. Its insignia, drawn by Major Pierre Charles L'Enfant, was a gold eagle, with an enamelled center emblematic of Cincinnatus, encircled by the motto of the society, "Omnia reliquit servare Republicam."

Marinus Willett was one of the charter members of the Society of the Cincinnati. Though he never held a major office, he was active in the New York chapter and frequently served on committees. On Independence Day each year the society marched and held banquets at which numerous toasts were drunk. The society, due to its limitation of membership to officers and its provision for hereditary membership, aroused much criticism. John Jay refused honorary membership, stating that he was "neither young enough nor old enough to deserve the honor." Thomas Jefferson said the society was "in opposition to the natural equality of man." John Adams called it "the deepest piece of cunning yet attempted." And old Ben Franklin though he accepted an honorary membership, poked fun at the society, calling its members "The Chevaliers of Cincinnatus." Marinus Willett, the defiant Son of Liberty, was living with strange companions, but one of them was his hero, George Washington, who had accepted the presidency of the National Society.

And Washington was now in New York, where he had been installed as President of the United States. The city took on a new social tone. Theaters reopened, despite the protests of the more puritanical elements. There were entertainments, balls and dinners to celebrate every auspicious occasion. Into this life walked Marinus Willett, erstwhile cabinet-maker. His companions were lawyers, statesmen and wealthy merchants. Many of them were college graduates. Willett, the hero of the frontier, was ill-equipped to cope with the minds and training of such men.

Peacemaker

SECRETARY OF WAR HENRY KNOX sent for Marinus Willett early in 1790. The Creek Indians were raising havoc along the border of Georgia. Three treaties had been signed between 1783 and 1786. The Creeks had declared them all invalid. Congress had notified them that should they persist in refusing to obey the treaties the United States would be forced to send troops to protect the frontier. James White, the Superintendent of Indian Affairs, had gone to see the Creek chiefs. The King of the Cowetas had told White that before his people gave up more land they would rather risk an attempt to get back the lands which had been taken from them. White had written Knox of "the natural reluctance of the Indians to part with any of their lands; to use their own expression, they look on their lands as their blood and life, which they must fight for rather than part with."

At the root of the trouble was Colonel Alexander McGillivray, a half-breed who had been deprived of his lands because of his father's participation in the late war. McGillivray, who possessed an English education, was a man of ambition. His resentment against the people of Georgia was unbounded. The chiefs of the hundred Creek villages were under the influence and direction of this remarkable man. Knox showed Willett a letter from McGillivray stating his defense of the Creeks:

"The gentlemen, my friends, do me justice when they inform you that I am desirous of peace. I have been now five years in laboring to bring about one with the State of Georgia, but in vain; more than a twelvemonth after the general peace was spent by us in representing to them, in friendly terms, the cruelty and injustice of their proceedings of wresting forcibly from us a large portion of our hunting lands, and which were in a great measure necessary for our support; that we were not situated as several other Indian nations were, with immense wildernesses behind us. On the contrary, we were surrounded from west to north by the Choctaws, Chickasaws, Cumberlands and Cherokees, and on every other side by the whites, so that our hunting grounds were already very insufficient for our purposes; to all of which we were always answered in haughty and contemptuous language, with threats to drive us over the Mississippi, so that having nothing to hope from their justice or humanity, it was resolved to raise up the red hatchet for self-preservation. As our cause was just, so fortune has favored our exertions in driving them from the contested ground. Though the war has reduced them to an extremity of distress yet their stubbornness of pride is such, that they take no measures to retract the conduct which has brought them to it; they have spurned every effort that Congress has offered at, to accommodate by its interference, the disputes between us. The new Congress will equally find them obstinate and intractable; the only method they can adopt, will be to leave the Georgians to their fate; and in another season 'tis probable that they will be brought to reason." The letter was dated January 4, 1789.

In September a commission of three, including General Lincoln, had spent $20,000 in a fruitless attempt to conciliate McGillivray, who had left the conference in a huff. All efforts to bring him back had failed, he pleading that he was feeling unwell and that the warriors had all gone hunting. The commissioners had attributed their failure to McGillivray's lack of co-operation.

Willett had read in the newspapers much of the story of the row between the Georgians and the Creeks. The Sons of Tammany had been agitating for some sort of conciliation. They thought that if McGillivray could be induced to come to New York, they could entertain him in Indian fashion and thus bring about a spirit of good-fellowship which might end in a lasting agreement. It would be necessary to send a representative who held the respect of the Indians and who was sympathetic with their problem. Knox had chosen Willett for the difficult task. Would he undertake the trip alone?

Marinus Willett, the good soldier, accepted.

He embarked on the sloop *Catharine* March 15, taking with him a servant and two horses. Willett, on his first real sea voyage, enjoyed the experience of sailing out of the harbor guided by a pilot and scooting before a light wind out of the west. It made a fellow hungry, so he cooked himself a hearty meal and went to bed. He slept well. For breakfast he enjoyed a beefsteak washed down with a bowl of tea. This trip was going to be bully.

Once on deck, with a fresh wind blowing in his face, he began to notice a perceptible motion, a rolling from side to side as the sloop rode waves which were tipped with white and which increased in size and power each moment. Some of the passengers rushed to the rail and hung over it. Willett drew his lips down in scorn. They remained in that position, for the colonel found something strange obstructing his stomach. He set his jaw. He clenched his fists. He who had been known as "The Devil" by the Indians on the frontier could not combat the terror which clutched at the pit of his stomach and brought beads of perspiration to a brow that was greenish-white. He retreated before the invisible foe, hurried below and threw himself on his bunk. Some of the dizziness left him but the revolt in his stomach broke forth afresh. He threw up, ingloriously.

Three days passed before he was able to crawl up on deck,

a hollow-cheeked shadow of the hero of Fort Stanwix. He landed at Charleston a week later, resolved in his mind that he had taken his last sea voyage, for he hadn't been able to eat a square meal for nine days. Marinus Willett enjoyed food.

Adam Gilchrist met him at the dock and provided excellent quarters for him in Charleston, where the colonel remained until April 2, making preparations for his journey. He set out on horseback, his servant following in a sulky loaded with baggage. One day on the trail satisfied the servant; with tears in his eyes he begged to be sent home and Willett was forced to comply. The colonel spent three days at Ninety Six with Ramsay and Goodwin, two lawyers who had married daughters of General Williamson. He was introduced to a German lad who had applied for service with him. Willett did not like the fellow's looks, but men willing to take a trek into the wilderness were scarcer than hens' teeth, so the young German rode behind the colonel to the plantation of General Andrew Pickens on the Seneca, a tributary of the Savannah River. Willett liked the general, whom he found to be "a decent and respectable gentleman." Here he met Young Corn, the lithe Indian who was to act as a guide through the Cherokee country. Young Corn, a member of that nation, had an "open, manly countenance." Willett placed trust in him from the start. On Monday, April 19 the party crossed the Seneca on Pickens' ferry, the general accompanying them to the opposite shore, where he said goodbye and invited Willett to stop with him on his return. The party took to the trail with Young Corn in the lead, followed by the colonel, then the loaded packhorse, with the German servant bringing up the rear.

The trip brought unpleasantries. After spending the night with Colonel Cleveland, the party wound their way through the forest. The bowhorse took fright, floundered off the trail, upset its load and injured its leg, so that only 24 miles were made that day. Willett became so provoked at some act of the young German that he "lost his center of gravity" and threw the lad into the fire. He recovered from his rage to find Young Corn staring at him with unbelieving eyes, while the servant, humbled, went about making chocolate. Willett, calmed by a cup of his favorite beverage, went to sleep and forgot about the incident.

The party arrived at Euestenaree, the sacred town of the Cherokees, on the 24th. Here all councils for settling of differences were held. It was also a town of refuge. Guilty ones fleeing from vengeance found safe haven here. No blood could be spilled at Euestenaree.

Willett met Colonel Alexander McGillivray at Oak Fusky on April 30. They had supper together and Willett delivered his letter from Knox. He found the Indian leader to be "a man of open, candid, generous mind, with good judgment and an excellent memory." McGillivray told him that the former attempts at settlement had been failures, but that he would try once more to bring about an adjustment of the relations between his people and the Georgia whites.

Willett attended "black drink" at Oak Fusky. Great kettles were set up in the center of the village. Rows of seats matted with reeds were arranged in a square, with openings at the angles for warriors to enter. The drink, made of a strong decoction of the kasina leaf, was boiled in the kettles. When it was ready a warrior went to a kettle and called in a loud voice for warriors to come and serve the company. He handed each warrior a bowl of the black drink. They drained the contents with ceremony. These warriors having received the drink from the chief warrior, they each took a bowl and stood in front of a member of the company. McGillivray raised the bowl to his lips but did not drink. Willett and other guests did likewise. The servers pealed forth two long drawn out notes which echoed from the hills. It was now time to drink. Into Willett's throat went the hot, acrid liquid. He wanted to choke but dared not. Bravely, with his face set, he downed his bowlful. He looked up to see McGillivray wrinkle a corner of one eye at him. They handed back the bowls and the warriors hurried on to serve their companions in arms. Speeches from old chiefs followed, long, eloquent harangues in the Indian manner, exhorting the warriors to perform their duties well.

McGillivray sent out ten "broken days" for his chiefs of the lower towns to meet at Ositchy in order to consult on Willett's business. The half-breed informed Willett that one stick was to be thrown away each day; when the sticks were all gone, the chief would know it was time for the meeting.

Willett spent the interval visiting with McGillivray and his wife at their home in Little Tallassee, dreaming on the banks of the Cousa or attending black drinks and Indian dances. He also walked to see the ruins of the old French Alabama fort.

The council at Ositchy was preceded by a black drink. Willett delivered a prepared speech to the "Brothers," saying that he had come to them from his Beloved Chief, George Washington, who was desirous of framing a treaty with them. The United States wanted none of their lands. The Beloved Chief wished to promote the trade and welfare of the Creek nation. He also invited them to send a delegation to New York to a great council fire that was to be kindled in that beloved town in order to "form a treaty which shall be strong as the hills and lasting as the rivers."

Willett retired. He was brought back in an hour to receive a lengthy and friendly reply from The Hallowing King, a fine-looking man and a great orator. Though the weather was hot and the road long, and though the last attempt at peace had resulted in failure, their Beloved Chief would go with Willett, and with him such chiefs and warriors as they would appoint for that purpose. Willett's trip had been a success.

On Saturday McGillivray invited his guest to an Indian ball play at a village five miles from Little Tallassee. Men, women and children had gathered around on an open field. Other Indians were arriving, some on foot, others on horseback. Here a maiden rode a fleet horse, her black tresses reaching to her waist, her streamers waving behind the tail of the horse. There a brave in all his finery galloped swiftly through the underbrush. All the important chiefs were present, their head-dresses shining above weather-beaten faces, their eyes focused upon the ends of the field, where the rival warriors were assembling for the contest.

The challenge had been made days before by one village to another. The previous night had been spent in dancing, drinking and ceremony. The players had been occupied all morning, painting and decorating their naked bodies as if preparing for the warpath. The time of their arrival on the field had been so contrived that they were now gathering in groups, eighty on a side, three hundred yards apart at the opposite ends of the clearing. Two poles were being erected at each end of the field; through these uprights the ball must pass in order to count one point. This task completed, the rival teams marched to the center of the field. The warriors held rackets in each hand. They singled out their opponents and placed their rackets against theirs. A ball was thrown high in the air. The game was on!

What a melee it was! One hundred and sixty warriors rushed around the field, trying to catch the ball in their rackets and fling it toward their opponents' goal. Willett could not stand still. This was something real. This was sport! He cheered when a dozen warriors tangled in a jumble of flailing arms, legs and rackets. His whole body tingled as one lithe warrior carried the ball in his racket, dodged three opponents and hurled it between the posts. Rougher and rougher became the play. Willett loved it.

All around him the spectators were mingling with each

other, arguing, laughing and placing large bets on the final result, the next goal, etc. McGillivray told Willett that at some of the ball plays the inhabitants of the losing village went home minus most of their clothes, ornaments and horses, hoping to regain them when they next hurled a challenge at some rival village. The women had a part, too. Armed with bottles and gourds, they watched every opportunity to quench the thirsts of their warriors. The women could be seen dodging among the players, their long hair streaming behind them, their faces flushed with excitement and exertion.

At last it was over. The challengers had lost. The victors rushed to collect the spoils. McGillivray touched Willett's sleeve and smiled. They must be getting on if they wished to start for New York on the morrow.

Mrs. McGillivray accompanied them several miles on their route north. Willett never forgot the fine-looking woman dressed in chintz skirt and white chemise; she sat straight as an arrow, her right hand holding the rein of a bridle decorated with silver plated buckles, her left hand grasping a silver mounted whip. "Her long, slender fingers, her delicate arms, her long hair from which flew a pair of streamers," Willett noted in his diary that night. "Perfection of nature's work. Indeed she is fair. Ah! most supremely fair." Willett was crowding fifty, but he had not lost interest in the fair sex.

Colonels Willett and McGillivray rode at the head of a procession which included two half-breed relatives of McGillivray, two servants and seven or eight warriors. Willett's servant brought up the rear with the bow and spare horses. The season was rainy. They travelled little one day when a hurricane blew steadily in their faces. They arrived at Stony Mountain, where they were met by an imposing array of Coweta and Cusetah chiefs and warriors. They crossed the Seneca on General Pickens' ferry and were received heartily by the general and chiefs and warriors from the Tallassees and Notches. The entire party left the Pickens estate on Friday, the 18th. Pickens rode with them for 15 miles, bade them bon voyage, and returned to his home.

The trip to New York was a series of celebrations. Richmond, where they rested three days, was enthusiastic in its welcome. At Fredericksburg the party was honored by a theater party and a public dinner. Willett was not able to visit Mount Vernon, though a messenger came to him with an invitation to visit Washington's home. He managed to pay his respects to Mrs. Lewis, the sister of his hero, and to spend a brief time at Washington's birthplace.

He and McGillivray were sitting in an inn at Guilford Court House when a woman dressed in black arrived unannounced, rushed up to McGillivray and cried on his shoulder. It was a Mrs. Brown who had been a prisoner among the Creeks, who had burned her home and killed her husband. McGillivray had restored her to her relatives.

The meeting distressed Willett. He confided to his diary: "To fly from such a scene was all that I could do. Cursed war thought I—and is the business I have left the friends of my heart and my home Intended to prevent catastrophys of this nature in futer. Happy truly happy shall I count myself if this should be the consequence. It will afford me more infinitly more satisfaction than I could possibly enjoy from the highest military atchievments." Truly, Willett was changing. He who once had sought the glories of war was now cursing the vehicle in which he had ridden to fame.

Once in this mood the colonel was convinced that the role of peacemaker was far superior to the work of a soldier. After an evening spent with a planter's family he became quite "lit'ry" in defense of his new role: "Dear rural hospitality! The antient Dominion of Virginia shall suffer no Dimunition by me. I will join with the honest throng that tell of they greatness. Peace be with you all. My mind is on the stretch for the blessings of a peace maker. Away ye triffling honors of a soldier. There was a time when I could toil and hazard much for you—But my face is now turned another way—a more delightfull way." And for the first time in years he remembered the poetic aspirations of his youth and wrote:

"Come sweetly smiling peace descend
And wave your downy wings
Each blessing on your train attend
Each joy around you springs."

The round of entertainment continued. At Gray's Ferry there came a messenger from the President and Council of the State of Pennsylvania, asking Willett to wait for their escort, which arrived with pomp and led the party into the City of Brotherly Love, where the party was treated with great courtesy. The Society of Friends visited Willett with a formal address. There was a public dinner and an evening at the theater. On Sunday Willett attended Christ Church both morning and evening.

New York opened its heart to the Creek Nation. A special barge met them at Elizabethtown Point on the morning of July 21. As it approached the Battery a federal salute was fired in its honor. The salute was repeated at Murray's Wharf, where the barge put in. A company of militia and the Society of Tammany in full regalia were drawn up on the wharf. The Creeks were stunned at the reception and puzzled by the hordes of white savages who swarmed around them, but they met the situation with their accustomed gravity.

Mrs. Adam Mappa, wife of an agent of the Holland Land Company, after witnessing the spectacle, wrote to her sister-in-law: "They are all savages, terrible to see, their natural colour black or inclining to be nearly black, they paint their faces with all sorts of colours, wear rings in their noses, and some have the border of the ear pierced and adorned with little tin plates. Moreover they deck themselves with feathers of all sorts and colours, and wear no breeches, so their backs are bare, and no agreeable sight."

The Creeks were escorted to the home of General Knox, who received them cordially and went with them to Washington's residence, where the President congratulated them on their safe arrival and expressed the hope that the coming interviews would result in benefits both to the Creeks and to the United States. After a visit to Governor Clinton the whole party was dined and feted at the City Tavern. The head table was graced by Knox, the senators and representative of Georgia, General Malcolm of the militia, Colonel Willett, Colonel McGillivray, sachems of Tammany and the three Creek kings. Seven toasts were drunk and the Creeks seemed highly pleased with such a polite and friendly reception.

Meanwhile the news of their arrival had been broadcasted throughout the city. The crowd at Murray's Wharf was nothing compared to the mobs which greeted the Indians every time they appeared in public. Captain Sarly of the ship *America,* lately from Canton, threw a real party which included such celebrities as Washington, Knox and Clinton. Tammany entertained at the Hall, where numerous toasts were drunk, songs were sung, and nine Indians did a tribal dance for their white brethren. St. Andrew's Society, not to be outdone by its rival, elected McGillivray to honorary membership.

The treaty with the Creeks was signed on August 17th. Among the signers were Knox, McGillivray, Willett and all the Creek chiefs. The provisions, in brief, were as follows:

1. The Creeks acknowledged themselves under the protection of the United States.
2. The Creeks would deliver up all prisoners.
3. The boundary would be established by a joint committee.
4. The United States guaranteed the Creeks their lands.

5. Any person trying to settle on the Creek lands could be punished by the Creeks.
6. There was to be no hunting by others on Creek lands.
7. The Creeks were to deliver up refugee Indians accused of crimes outside Creek lands.
8. Whites entering Creek lands and committing crimes were subject to the same jurisdiction as in the state from which they came.
9. There was to be no retaliation by the Creeks until satisfaction had been asked and refused.
10. The United States promised to assist the Creeks with animals and implements to improve husbandry.

The Creeks, apparently satisfied, departed for home. Marinus Willett's job was done. One of the most difficult problems of the country had been settled. How long? Willett did not know, but he hoped the treaty would be lasting.

The ink had hardly dried when the State of Georgia, through its Governor, was issuing a proclamation warning the Creeks against going into the State armed until "the pleasure of the President of the United States be known respecting ravages made." A white lad had been murdered on land belonging to the whites. A body of Georgia troops had attacked the Creeks and had been overwhelmed; some had been massacred.

Willett received a letter from McGillivray while the uproar in Georgia was at its peak. McGillivray told of his trip home in the rain through swampy country. A murder had been committed during his absence. A Cusitah had been killed by a Georgian. The Indians had demanded revenge. They had waited four months without getting a reply from Georgia, so they had taken satisfaction by killing a young lad on the frontier. They had acted under orders of The Bird Tail King. The storm had blown over but "God only knows how long the present calm will last. I will, perhaps, be not credited when I observe, that the upper Georgians never will suffer satisfaction to be given for killing an Indian; and, indeed, every month affords instances of felons among them being rescued from justice, when condemned for the most atrocious offences."

Marinus Willett had travelled 2800 miles to carry his mission through to a happy conclusion. He had undergone considerable hardship. The government had expended huge sums of money. And now the Georgians would not co-operate.

There was one thing for which the colonel was thankful. He had learned that the good sloop *Catharine* had been lost on Ocracook Island on her next trip out of New York for Charleston.

Burrite

UNHAPPY YEARS LAY IN STORE for Marinus Willett. Mary died in the summer of 1793 and was buried in Trinity graveyard. Edward Willett passed away on December 8, 1794. Cedar Grove was no longer a home; it was merely a beautiful house on the East River. Willett felt the need of a companion. An attractive widow, Susanna Vardle, was the toast of the city. Willett wooed and won her. Trinity Church was the scene of the wedding.

Susanna came to Cedar Grove in high spirits but soon became dissatisfied, for she wished to be in the midst of the social whirl and found Cedar Grove too isolated. Furthermore she had a will of her own. Willett, accustomed to having his own way, resented her interference in household matters. As a result Susanna spent her days in the city, where she gossiped about her husband in the homes of friends, and even stopped acquaintances on the street in order to air her grievances against the colonel.

George Clinton was fighting for his political life against John Jay, Federalist candidate for Governor. One William Willcox, who had once been Willett's friend, was a rabid Federalist. During the heat of the campaign he and Willett had words in a tavern. Willett challenged him to a duel. The two veterans took a few shots at each other in order to satisfy their respective prides. Fortunately the aim of both men seemed to be poor. Clinton nosed out Jay and Willett once more became High Sheriff.

He left New York in the summer of 1796 and travelled for a month through New England, keeping a diary of his observations. He was particularly impressed with the fisheries at Marblehead and the shoe industry at Lynn. He toured New Hampshire and attended commencement at Dartmouth College. Late in August he visited Greenfield, Northampton and Pittsfield. He waxed enthusiastic about the canal which ran beside the Connecticut River at South Hadley. The Boston Mail Stage carried him through the Berkshires to Albany and the Mohawk Valley.

A week was spent in the area so dear to his heart. He visited Fort Plain, where he met old companions of the war. He also stopped at Whitestown, where Colonel Jacob Sanger met him and rode with him on horseback to Fort Stanwix, around whose ruins a thriving settlement had sprung up. He would have lingered at Stanwix but a heavy rain set in and it seemed advisable to go back down the Valley. He spent the night at Old Fort Schuyler and left the next morning for Schenectady and New York.

He was back in the Mohawk Valley the following spring to inspect his land holdings. He spent nearly three months and left a short account of his trip:

"On Fryday the last of March Left N. York and on Monday April 3 at 2 oClock P M arrived at Albany after a pleasant passage. Tuesday May 9th left Albany at 3 oC P M arrived in the evening at Schenectidy. Set out in the Whitestown stage the next morning and on Thursday evening arrived at Fort Schuyler. Saturday 13th went to the Unadalla. Lodged that night at Cars & the next at Simmons. Visited my lotts in the 17th, 18th and 19th Townships. Lodged two Nights in Mr. Morgans house at Brookfield occupied by Mr. Palmer and returned on Thursday evening to Mr. Hous's at Fort Schuyler. Thursday 25th went to Paris and returned the Saturday following to Fort Schuyler. Thursday June 1st went to the German Flatts in a boat remained at Mr. Aldriges untill Monday. Then took the Stage and arrived at Schenectidy on Tuesday at 3 oClock P M. And on Wednesday morning June 7th went to Albany in a stage. Wednesday 14th June left Albany for New York by water by Captain Morus Roffs sloop and arrived at New York between 12 & one oClock Saturday Morning 17th."

He returned to face a divorce suit which he did not contest. Susanna was granted a separation. Cedar Grove was put up for sale but there were no purchasers.

Willett had long been an admirer of Aaron Burr, the little lawyer who, through political intrigue, had gained such prominence that the Republicans ran him with Thomas Jefferson in an effort to break Federalism in the White House. Burr, sensing that New York might be the key state in the election, enlisted the aid of the Sons of Tammany. Though he and Willett were never members of this organization, their friends, Matthew L. Davis, William Van Ness and the Swartwouts were all Sachems. Political meetings held at Martling's Tavern at the corner of Nassau and George Streets brought out the plebeian elements of the city, house-to-house workers who, through personal contact with voters, overcame Alexander Hamilton's oratory and carried, not only the city but the state for the Republican party.

Burr went on to fight for the Presidency against Jefferson, a maneuver which brought him the condemnation of the Clintonians as well as the Federalists. When he was defeated in the United States Senate, most of his friends left him.

Willett clung to Burr, for he believed that the little politician had been in the right. He lent Burr money to pay his debts and was a frequent visitor at Richmond Hill, Burr's mansion on the North River.

Meanwhile Willett surprised New York society by taking unto himself a third wife. Margaret Bancker, daughter of a close friend, was twenty-four and the colonel lacked one year of sixty. Cedar Grove was re-opened. Children came to bless the union. Four boys and a girl were born between 1800 and 1810. They were named Marinus, William Marinus, Edward Marinus, Elbert Marinus and Margaret. Evidently the mother had a word to say when it came to naming the only girl. Cedar Grove became a gathering place for friends and a playground for the children of the neighborhood. There was swimming from the ferry pier and boating on the East River. The spacious gardens made an ideal playground for the youngsters. These promised to be happy years for Marinus Willett.

Aaron Burr was to ruin them. The little politician, knowing that he was through as a national figure, decided to gain for himself the Governorship of New York. Marinus Willett, together with Anthony Lispenard and John Rathbone, signed the following petition: "In discharge of the duty imposed on us by the inclosed resolution, we take the liberty of soliciting your support of Aaron Burr as Governor at the coming election, upon the result of which we believe the welfare of the state especially depends. A dangerous aristocracy has arisen and by means of wealth, of family connections, and of offices, has acquired a power and influence, which ought to alarm every friend of Republican principles, this combination if not now resisted may rise above our control."

"The dangerous aristocracy," consisting of the Clintons, the Livingstons, the Republican regulars, plus the entire Federal party backed by Alexander Hamilton, nominated Morgan Lewis, a member of an aristocratic family, as Burr's opponent.

The Lewis backers enlisted the aid of James Cheetham, publisher of the *New York American Citizen* and pusher of the most vitriolic pen ever to be used in the New York press. Cheetham dubbed Burr "a Cataline, a debauchee, a liar and a monster." The Burrites brought out a paper, *The Corrector,* to combat the epithets of Cheetham, who replied by intimating that Burr kept a seraglio and chose to be a Solomon with three hundred wives and concubines.

The Burrites, supported by the Martling Men, managed to carry the city for Burr, but Lewis won the state by over 8000 votes.

The Society of the Cincinnati met on the fourth of July each year to celebrate the anniversary of the Declaration of Independence. The meeting in 1804 was charged with dynamite, for both Burr and Hamilton were present. Willett noticed that Burr raised his head when spoken to but made no attempt at conversation. Hamilton, on the other hand, was nervous and talkative. It had been the custom for Hamilton, between toasts, to sing "The Drum," a song which had grown out of the war. The request was made by the chairman.

Hamilton rose. "If you will excuse me," he said, "I would prefer not to sing this year."

The gathering shouted him down.

"Very well," said the Federalist, "you shall have it."

He sang the song, though Willett noticed that his voice lacked the enthusiasm of former years. Hamilton looked tired. He had never been a man who exercised. His body was soft and paunchy. He seemed glad when the song was over.

Events moved to a swift climax. They culminated in Burr's challenge to a duel and in Hamilton's reluctant acceptance.

Marinus Willett rode out to Richmond Hill early on that fateful July morning. Billy Van Ness, Matt Davis and John Swartwout were already there. Burr lay asleep on a couch. He evidently had retired late, for he had merely removed his coat and shoes. Six blue boxes containing letters rested on a table at his side.

Burr awoke. He donned a black bombaseen coat, said to have been made specially for the occasion. He had little to say. Van Ness, who was to be Burr's second, gave orders to the others. Swartwout was to remain at Richmond Hill; he was to carry the news of the result of the duel to the city. Willett and Davis were to accompany Burr and his second to Weehawk, three miles above Richmond Hill, on the Jersey side of the river. They were to conceal themselves in the bushes and witness the duel.

Though the morning was clear Van Ness carried an umbrella in addition to the pistol case. The four men stepped into a barge which was rowed across the Hudson. They climbed the heights, being careful not to disturb "The Captain," a recluse who had a hut there. Willett and Davis took their places in the bushes, choosing a point from which they could observe the duel accurately.

Hamilton arrived, accompanied by Nat Pendleton, his second, who entered into negotiations with Van Ness. Lots were cast for position. Hamilton won the right to fight with the sun at his back. The pistols were loaded and the men took their stations ten paces apart.

"Present!"

Two pistols sounded in rapid succession. Hamilton slumped to the ground. Burr advanced toward his fallen adversary with a gesture of regret. Without speaking he and Van Ness withdrew, for the sound of shots had brought Dr. Hossack running to the scene and Burr did not wish to be recognized. The Burrites jumped into their barge and were rowed back to Richmond Hill.

"Oh Burr, oh Burr, what hast thou done,
Thou hast shooted dead great Hamilton!
You hid behind a bunch of thistle,
And shooted him dead with a great hoss pistol!"

Burr and Van Ness did not wait to face the music. They fled from the city. Willett and Davis were arrested. They refused to testify against Burr and were allowed to cool their heels in jail. They were released when the jury declared Burr guilty of willful murder and named Van Ness and Pendleton as accessories. Burr hurried toward the South, his mind filled with grandiose schemes, but he had lost forever the admiration and loyalty of Marinus Willett.

Mayor

WILLETT, WHO HAD TEETERED on the political tightrope for years, threw in his lot with Morgan Lewis, who held office through a coalition of Republicans and Federalists.

The Clintonians, unhappy under the coalition, decided to unseat Lewis. DeWitt Clinton consulted with Dr. Peter Irving, with the result that 68 members of the Clinton and Burr factions ate supper at Dyde's Tavern. Toasts were given to Thomas Jefferson, George Clinton and Aaron Burr, the last-named receiving more cheers than the other two, much to the embarrassment of the Clintonians. Conditions of agreement between the two factions involved the recognizing of Burr as a Republican, the stilling of Cheetham's poisonous pen and the placing of the Burrites on the same footing with the Clintonians.

All might have gone well, except that radical Republicans who were not invited gathered at Martling's Tavern on February 25, 1806 to denounce the proposed union, stating that "Aaron Burr does not possess the confidence of the Republican party."

The Clintonians had been blocked temporarily. Morgan Lewis, from his stronghold in Albany, began to oust the followers of DeWitt Clinton in New York City. The Clintonian newspapers caught fire. Thomas Farmer printed a series of scathing articles in his *Republican Watch Tower*, accusing Lewis of being "in league with the Federalists and endeavouring to dessiminate jealousy and prejudice between the republicans of the state and to place one district in hostile array to another." He bared the Governor to the skeleton and even picked at his bones. Lewis, in a fit of rage, sued Farmer for $100,000 damages.

DeWitt Clinton, then Mayor of the city, was the recipient of abuse penned by one "Brutus." Clinton, after tracing the articles to their source, sued Matthew L. Davis for slander. Burr's friend, pleading not guilty, was successfully defended by two Federalist lawyers. Clinton swallowed the pill bitterly. And on February 14, 1807 the Council at Albany voted unanimously "that DeWitt Clinton be removed as mayor of New York." The Clintons had been ousted at last.

Suddenly, like a bolt out of the blue, came the news that young Samuel Swartwout was in prison in New Orleans. He had come to General James Wilkinson with a letter from Aaron Burr. Swartwout had offered the general $100,000 if he would co-operate with the conspirators. The crafty Wilkinson had stalled for four days, until he had wormed out of Swartwout the details of Burr's plans, then he had clapped the New Yorker in jail. Rumor had it that Swartwout would be sent to Washington for trial. Late in February the New York papers carried the news that Colonel Burr had been captured near Natchez. He had surrendered without resistance. The jig was up, and he knew it.

This was ambrosia and nectar to the Republican press, especially in view of the fact that the chief political plum, the Mayoralty of New York, was to be filled by Lewis. This nonelective position paid no regular salary but the emoluments derived from other sources were considerable. For example, the market fees went to His Honor, who turned over half of them to the Common Council. This august body, not to be outdone in generosity, conceded three-tenths of the revenue from tavern licenses to their benefactor. It was a pleasing little game, completely satisfying to both Mayor and Council.

Times were changing, however. The Council thought that the Mayor was getting much the better of the bargain. He should have a fixed salary and refuse all other emoluments. Was this new scheme consistent with the City Charter? Some of the newspapers thought otherwise and the wrangle continued.

There was much speculation in the Republican press as to DeWitt Clinton's successor. It was obvious to the editors that no appointee of Lewis could be honest, and the Republicans were prepared to denounce any candidate the Governor might suggest. Lewis kept his tongue in his cheek and let the opposition make conjectures, which they did, willingly. To their ears had come the shocking news that Tommy Storm was to be appointed. Could it be possible "that the Council would commit upon this city so great an outrage?" Wrong guess. Lewis was not to send Storm, but had chosen Smith Thompson, Judge of the Supreme Court, "a branch of the Governor's family by affinity and a *quid*." Thompson, in addition to being a Burrite, had never been a resident of New York City, and by the City Charter was not eligible. The Clintonians, knowing that Lewis could get around that technicality, published scathing editorials under the heading, "Our Albany Mayor." Thompson, who could not see relinquishing a secure post to be cast into the sea of city politics, refused the appointment.

The Clintonians were puzzled. Whom would Lewis appoint? Would he dare to give the plum to his son-in-law, Maturin Livingston? The papers played with the idea for several days, knifing at the Governor's vulnerable points. Lewis appointed Livingston to the post of City Recorder.

The Clintonians, reluctant to leave their speculations, were booming Daniel Tompkins for the Governorship against Lewis when, late in the evening of March 13th, the harbor master brought with him a commission appointing Marinus Willett Mayor of New York City.

Marinus Willett? It was unbelievable. He was "seventy-four years old with one foot in the grave." The colonel was in his "second childhood."

Ah, a technicality! Was the old warrior constitutionally eligible to hold the office? The Clintonians knew Willett was "Intellectually and otherwise unfit." By the Charter, the Mayor was first judge of the Court of Common Pleas, and held that job under good behavior until he "shall have attained the age of sixty." What a laugh on Lewis! Marinus Willett was "seventy-four."

The humorists found the colonel excellent material. Their quips were barbed and occasionally dipped in vitriol. "Willett fill the mayor's chair? I think not. But what may we not expect from folly and a vindictive spirit?" "Willett, our *mare*, was on the eve of the Revolution, it is said, a *shoemaker*. A good shoemaker is an useful and meritorious citizen —but would it not have been to his credit and advantage if he had been *kept to the last?*" "Is it not strange that Governor Lewis, after hunting two or three weeks among his *jackasses* for a *mare* should at last pitch on the Town *Bull?*"

The poets also had their inning at the expense of the colonel. One wrote:

"Can such things be
And overcome us like a summer's cloud,
Without our special wonder?
Can you behold such sights
And keep the natural ruby of your cheeks?"

William Coleman, editor of the *Evening Post,* did not resort to flippancy. *The Post,* a Lewis paper, was boosting the Governor for re-election. Coleman based his criticism of Willett upon "personal incompetency." Willett was not a lawyer. He was not even versed in law reading. Yet the Mayor would be expected to preside over the civil and criminal tribunals, to deliver up charges to the Grand Jury, to sum up cases for the petit jury and to determine questions of evidence upon the trial. It was absurd to expect satisfaction from Willett, "a gentleman who had probably never looked into a law book in his life, and whose habits and pursuits have not been, we believe, at any time, such as to render him conversant with letters." The Mayor was expected, as chief police officer, to take charge at all disturbances, riots and fires and to answer any alarm of danger. How could a man of Willett's age possibly perform these tasks? Coleman put the question squarely up to Willett. He hoped that the colonel would resign the office, for the appointment was "one of the most unfortunate that could have been made," an opinion in which he had found "all men of all parties agreed."

Marinus Willett did not take Coleman's advice. He appeared at Federal Hall at four o'clock on March 16th and made his way to the Mayor's office. The old warrior knew this room well. Hadn't he appeared there often during his years as High Sheriff? Hadn't he sat with the Council for a year way back in '89? Now he had been chosen to preside over that unruly body.

He marched forward as if to battle. He found his way impeded, not by an enemy host, but by admirers who had crowded in to see the hero of Fort Stanwix take office as Mayor of the city. The passageways were completely blocked. It was impossible to reach the office where the Council usually sat. The tall colonel found himself encircled by well-wishers. He could make no progress, so the large courtroom was opened and the crowd pressed toward it; in a few moments it was filled.

Willett and the Council filed in and took their seats. The clerk rose and read the commission: "His Excellency the Governor by and with the advice of the Council of Appointment has pleased to appoint Marinus Willett, Esqr. to the Office of the Mayor of this City."

The oath was administered before a hushed gathering; then the plaudits of the crowd rang out. Willett rose and bowed acknowledgment. He said, "I have been selected by the Council of Appointment for the office of Mayor, without any solicitation on my part, or on the part of any of my friends, within my knowledge. I feel a confidence that, with the aid of the Board, I shall be enabled to discharge the duties of the office. Believing as I do that, next to the faithful preaching of the gospel, the due administration of justice is one of the greatest blessings a free people can enjoy, I shall endeavour to square my conduct in such a manner as to do strict justice to all."

He sat down to the plaudits of the people. There were also several audible hisses.

Peter Irving, who had kept a discreet silence during the innuendoes of Cheetham and Farmer and the contemptuous advice of Coleman, gave birth to eulogies in his *Morning Chronicle*. "Joy seemed to beam in every countenance," he wrote in describing the scene, "and enthusiasm glowed in every bosom, on beholding the war-worn soldier of our country, the companion, the friend and the fellow-sufferer of our immortal Washington, invested with the authority to administer those laws for which he had so ably and so honorably fought, in the 'days that tried men's souls!' That is the man, fellow-citizens, that Cheetham, a renegade, and a wanderer on the face of the earth, is villifying and abusing. If Col. Willett has, in the distant parts of the state, one *old whig* friend, whose soul will not shrink and recoil from the characters who patronize this wretch, in such outrageous attacks, that friend is unworthy of being longer enrolled in the long list of worthies, that by their blood and treasure established our independence."

Supporters took up the cudgel in Willett's behalf. One defender answered the arguments of the Clintonians regarding age, infirmity and Burrism. Willett was seven years, five months and five days younger than the Vice President, George Clinton; his paralysis was precisely now what it had been during the Revolution, when he made the sortie from Fort Stanwix (the writer spelled it Stanwich); surely, he had been a Burrite, but so had Daniel Tompkins, the Cheetham candidate for Governor. "Had the angel Gabriel been appointed, it would, to these *virtuous* citizens, have been exactly the same thing."

Cheetham slapped back, but was pretty well silenced when Irving remarked that Willett had aided in giving the state a world for "such a viperous little knot of modern heroes, wherein to strut and cringe." And the day after his induction into office the Mayor gave lie to the accusations that he was a dog who could be led around. A "fluttering magpie" halted the colonel on the street and demanded that he remove a certain person in order to make room for a partisan office-seeker. Willett straightened to his full height, focused his eyes upon the "magpie" and bellowed, "I will make no removals to please puppies!"

The duties of Mayor were numerous. He presided at the Common Council meetings, but had no vote unless a tie resulted. He issued warrants on the city treasurer when authorized by the Council. He was the presiding judge of the Court of General Sessions and occasionally acted as judge of the Mayor's Court, though that duty had been taken over by the Recorder in 1803. He was also a member of the Court of Oyer and Terminer. His powers of appointment were great. He also acted as clerk of the markets and granted all tavern licenses. In these capacities he received fees which netted him a tidy sum each year. He still received no fixed salary, but his emoluments from fees amounted to between $5,000 and $8,000 a year.

The new Mayor was conscious of his limitations. Not being a man of law, he could not judge cases with the cleverness which had characterized his predecessors. He would not attempt to pose as an expert on legal matters, so a deputy mayor was sworn in to handle this part of the job. This act brought a laugh from the Clintonians, but much of the sting had gone from their adders. The physical side of the office, involving the supervising of police and fire departments, Willett felt perfectly capable to handle. Hadn't he served as High Sheriff in the most turbulent period of the city's history?

In addition to the countless petitions involving land disputes, wharf repairs, the almshouse, cleaning and paving streets, fire protection, etc., he had to contend with a Gubernatorial election and a European War, two events which were curiously intertwined with the dissentions of the Republican party. And in the background the trial of Aaron Burr at Richmond staggered through the entire summer, every proceeding being recorded intact in the several New York papers, while the editors either vilified or defended Burr, according to their political leanings.

Morgan Lewis was up for re-election as Governor. His opponent, sponsored by the Clintonians, was Daniel Tompkins, once leagued with Burr. The Federalists, puzzled by the complications, chose Lewis as the lesser of two evils and joined him in the American Party, a group whose sole reason for allegiance was hatred for DeWitt Clinton. The American Party was composed of "Federalists, Burrites, Lewisites or quids, and men of colour." Its sympathies in the European War were with Great Britain. Tompkins and the Clintonians, on the other hand, were backed by all Republicans who loved France and also by the Irish who were now seeking citizenship in the United States after their unsuccessful revolt against British tyranny. Among the sons of Erin who had landed in New York was Thomas Addis Emmett, brother of the Irish patriot. Emmett, a hater of all things British, wrote with such a poisonous pen that Peter Irving dubbed him "Adder" Emmett. Thomas Paine also came out of retirement to aid Thomas Farmer in defending himself against Lewis in the slander suit.

The American Party, termed the British faction by their opponents, asked the New Yorkers if they would be Jacobins, deists and atheists, or free people and Christians. The Clintonians replied that if Lewis were re-elected the people of New York would have to aid England in her wars; press gangs would overrun the city; stamp taxes and land taxes would be levied; "even the light of heaven would be taxed with a gag law to prevent murmurs." The day before the election began *The Republican Watch Tower* threw out its final appeal to the Irish vote: "Irishmen! Catholics! in opposing the *British Party*, you support the cause of Republicanism, of Religion, and of God."

The polls opened at ten o'clock on May 1st. For three days the rival factions manipulated the polling places to the best of their respective abilities. Strong-arm squads were used to intimidate voters. When the storm had blown over the Lewisites had carried New York City, but the upstate counties had clung to the Clintonian banner. Daniel Tompkins was elected Governor. Willett knew that his term as Mayor would end at the close of the next January.

The closing days of June produced a broadside which left strong reverberations in New York City. The British man-of-war *Leopard* had halted the United States frigate *Constitution* and had demanded of Commodore Barron the release of three sailors. Barron had refused to muster his men for examination, whereupon the *Leopard* had levelled several broadsides at the defenseless frigate, killing three men and wounding eighteen.

War seemed imminent. New York stood in immediate danger of attack. What had the Mayor been doing to prevent invasion by sea? Nothing, concluded his opponents. But they were wrong. The Council had been co-operating with the national government. On July 13 it ceded "such parts of the public grounds at the Battery and at the Basin on Duane Street as were deemed necessary for the defence of the city." Colonel Jonathan Williams was working on a plan for fortifying the harbor at The Narrows. The national government was improving the forts on Governor's Island.

The Williams plan advocated the sinkings of numerous blocks 50 feet square at The Narrows. These blocks, with their tops 10 feet below water level, were to be armed with chevaux-de-frise. These fortifications would cost in the neighborhood of $1,000,000 but the seriousness of the emergency required such an outlay.

Thomas Paine, expert at all things, became an authority on fortifications. He wrote: "This most certainly would prevent Hostile Ships coming to the city, and it is equally certain it would prevent the tide coming up and lay the wharves at New York dry, and be the ruin of all the towns on the North River that depend for commerce on tide water." Cheetham chided Paine on his "tide theory," whereupon Paine called Cheetham "a splenetic John Bull."

Willett had an idea. The obstructions could be run in different lines from either shore, so that although each line of blocks might be half the width of The Narrows, the extremities would be 100 yards distant from each other, in the line of the current, thus leaving a lane for American ships when passage was not closed by a chain. No new chain would have to be purchased; one was lying at West Point in good condition. The Willett plan would cut expenses to $327,600.

The national government had not been idle. The works on Governor's Island had been enlarged and a powerful battery was being erected. The government also planned works at Ellis Island and the Battery, also a block in the North River off Duane Street.

The Council accepted the Williams report, limiting the cost to $200,000, which they planned to cover through an issue of corporation bonds. The Council did not doubt but what the national government would assume the debt; if not, the city could pay it in three years by doubling the yearly taxes. Willett wrote to the Secretary of War and the Council sent a memorial to Congress, asking for an appropriation for harbor defense. The Secretary replied that there would be "no indisposition on his part to the extension of the means of defense for the harbor and the city of New York when cessation of the bed of the harbor be made by the legislature of the state and necessary funds be provided by Congress." The Council petitioned the legislature and there the matter rested when Willett left office.

New York was not attacked, but the Embargo Act rebounded on the city with full force. Ships were tied up in port. Hundreds of seamen roamed the city, discontented, grumbling. With winter coming on, what was to become of them? They couldn't sail on ships. The city had no employment for them. Early in January, 1808 the seamen called a meeting in the Park and had the announcements printed in the newspapers.

Marinus Willett had never been a defensive fighter. He issued a proclamation: "The Mayor decidedly disapproves the mode of application recommended in a morning paper, to be pursued by the Sailors of this port for relief. He informs the public that the Corporation will, in the present emergency, as they have done on former occasions, provide for the wants of every person, without distinction, who may be considered proper objects of relief. The Mayor cannot conclude this Notice, without exhorting all classes of Citizens to refrain from assembling in the mode as proposed, and especially dissuades the Sailors from meeting in the park."

He rode to the Park, formerly The Fields, where he had on so many occasions been a leader in the revolts of the Sons of Liberty. Now he was the upholder of the existing law and order. It must have seemed strange to him, but he handled the situation well. He accepted the sailors' memorial and read it carefully. The embargo had destroyed employment by sea. It was impossible to gain work ashore. What had America to boast of but her agriculture and her commerce? The destruction of one would be the ruin of the other. The sailors were in debt. Should they plunder, thieve and rob? If so, the prison would be their certain doom. They were not objects of pity yet. They wanted employment.

The Mayor was familiar with such pleas. He had heard them from soldiers who had appeared in rags to plead for pay that was long overdue from an impoverished Congress. He had worked indefatigably to help the men who had suffered with him on the frontier. Wasn't there a parallel in the cases of these sailors? Willett thought so. He tucked the memorial into his pocket and made a brief speech, assuring the sailors that the Corporation would take their memorial into consideration. The crowd dispersed and the Mayor rode back to his office.

Willett kept his promise. He could not secure employment for the sailors in the city, but he wrote to Captain Chauncey of the United States Navy, stationed in the Navy Yard. Would Chauncey take the men if the Corporation paid for their maintenance? Chauncey would be glad to oblige the Mayor. Thus the city was rid of the unemployed sailors.

The embargo affected more than the sailors. Business declined. Hundreds were thrown out of employment. Willett tried public works as a method of creating employment. The Collect was being filled and men were employed to load the carts. Others were employed in regulating and filling the streets near Corlear's Hook, evidently a concession to the Mayor's own real estate plans. These projects did not alleviate the misery. The almshouse was full and a soup kitchen had to be established there. Three days a week rations of soup, bread and beef were issued and on Saturdays a half pound of pork and a pint of beans per individual.

All was not unpleasant, however. Robert Fulton, after his

successful trip up the Hudson River in the *Clermont*, was granted the freedom of the city in a gold box. On Evacuation Day Willett and the Council reviewed the parade which wound through the city. In answer to a petition from his rival, De Witt Clinton, Willett and the Council asked the state to cede the arsenal to the Corporation for the use of the New York Public Free School, on condition that the trustees agree to educate the children belonging to the almshouse free of charge.

News came on September 3 that Aaron Burr had been acquitted of high treason. Willett, disgusted with the whole affair, probably agreed with Coleman's pithy remark: "We have scotch'd the snake, Not killed it."

During the nine months that Willett filled the Mayor's chair, he and the Council had been working on a code of law for the city. It was published in January, 1808, just before Governor Tompkins removed Willett and returned De Witt Clinton as Mayor of New York City.

The Ferry War

Willett returned to private life at Cedar Grove, where he could now attend to several matters which had been distressing him for several years.

Abraham Cannon had been a resident of Corlear's Hook for over 50 years. In addition to operating an inn he was the owner of a ferry which plied back and forth occasionally between his wharf at the foot of Grand Street and Long Island. His ferry was a rowboat affair which was neither comfortable nor dependable. Cannon also showed little interest in developing the section, being content to run his inn and ferry. Willett, enthusiastic about his property, wished to see the countryside developed into a residential section. He thought that a better ferry service should be established between Manhattan and Long Island. The Stuyvesants were of the same opinion, so two petitions were sent to the Common Council in 1802, requesting permission to establish ferries to Bushwick, one from the Stuyvesant land, the other from Willett's property. The ferries were authorized on condition that the petitioners grant lots upon which ferryhouses and wharves could be built by the city.

Cannon woke up with a start. It is also possible that Mangle Minthorne, alderman from the Seventh Ward, had a finger in the pie. A petition was sent in by one Thomas Morrell of Bushwick, asking permission to establish a ferry from his land to that of Cannon at the foot of Grand Street. The

Council tabled the petition while a committee conferred with Willett. They were somewhat apprehensive about the value of such a ferry, for it would involve the expense of constructing a ferryhouse and wharves at a spot which was on the outskirts of the city. It did not seem that a lessee would be able to pay rent equal to the interest on the money to be expended. Would the colonel take over the lease for six years without rent on condition that he pay for the construction of the ferryhouses and wharves? The colonel would be glad to do so and would agree to return them to the city in good condition at the end of six years. The committee recommended to the Council that the ferry be built under those conditions. Two large boats should be provided to carry horses, cattle and bulky articles; two smaller ships would suffice for passengers, who would be required to pay six cents for passage, a somewhat higher rate than that charged on the Brooklyn ferries. The lease was made out to Willett and the ferry was constructed and set in motion.

In that summer of 1803 Mangle Minthorne came up for re-election as alderman of the Seventh Ward. Willett, who had been inspector of elections in the ward for several years, was once more appointed. The Council's orders stated definitely that the election would be held at the Presbyterian Church in East Rutgers Street. Willett, after receiving his notice of appointment, made his usual preparations, such as appointing a clerk and preparing his poll book. On election day the clerk came hurrying to Willett, saying that Colonel Rutgers had refused to permit the Corporation to use the church for election purposes. Willett hurried to the scene to find a group of bystanders outside the locked church. He went to Rutgers, who told him that he would not open the church but that he had provided a small tenement nearby in which to hold the election, which resulted in a defeat for Minthorne.

De Witt Clinton, who was Mayor at the time, sent a committee to see Willett, who informed them of the circumstances surrounding the election. At the next meeting of the Council the report of the committee was read and a vote taken. Led by Minthorne, the aldermen voted the election null and void and refused to seat the winning candidate. A second election was held with a different inspector in charge. Minthorne was elected.

The Willett ferry operated during the summer of 1804, but ran into difficulties during the ensuing winter, which was exceptionally severe. Ice formed at Woodhull's landing. A reef caused a detour even in good weather. Unfavorable tides handicapped the passage. The distance was too great. The ferry catered to the few rather than to the general public. Willett discovered these complaints when the opposition in July, 1805, through the medium of a committee from the new Council, recommended that another ferry be constructed from Abraham Cannon's property to the land of Thomas Morrell in Bushwick.

Arguments in favor of the new ferry were many. Grand Street was the widest thoroughfare in the section, with more streets radiating out of it than from any other. The new market would probably be established there and the ferry and market should be close together. Morrell's Point had been free from ice despite the severe winter. The distance was shorter. No tide interfered. No reef menaced the boats. Willett and Woodhull had no reason to believe that their ferry had a permanent monopoly. The Council could not commit itself to an inferior ferry forever. Furthermore Mr. Cannon had kept a ferry for 50 years. The new Council, of which Minthorne was a prominent member, recommended that the new ferry be built, under the same conditions in which Willett and Woodhull had leased the rights; if the latter ferry should be discontinued by the Council, the property would be restored to Willett and his partner.

The fight continued for several months. Witnesses were

examined and much talking was done by both sides. The Council finally voted to permit Cannon and Morrell to build their ferry and also extended the lease of Willett and Woodhull for six more years after the expiration of their original rights. The first battle between Willett and Cannon had ended in a draw.

The second round followed closely upon the heels of the first. A stretch of low, marshy land lay at the end of Broome Street, where Cannon's property met Cedar Grove. In 1806 the city had built a bulkhead between the two properties, but that had not settled the argument. The water continued to ebb and flow through the low area, filling it with refuse and filth. Cannon thought that Willett should fill up the declivity, but the colonel felt that the chief part of the job resolved upon his neighbor. He refused to budge. Cannon sued him, with no result. In desperation Cannon sent a long petition to the Council which had been so helpful to him in establishing his ferry. The Council did not care for the role of arbiter. If they ordered one man to fill up his land, the water would rush in and commence filling the other man's property. There was no way of determining how much dirt each contender should throw into the declivity. The Council tossed the job into the lap of the street commissioner, who engaged men and filled the disputed hollow, while Willett and Cannon glared at each other from their respective heights. Would the second round end in a draw, or would there be a knockout by one side or the other?

The answer came in October, when the grading had been completed and the water shut out from the disputed land. Willett received his share of the bill, $73.05. Cannon must have fainted on the spot, for his share was $323.95.

The ferry war continued unabated. Here the advantage lay with Cannon. The distance was shorter, the trip was less impeded by tides and reefs, and in the winter Morrell's Point was free from ice. By 1813 the colonel was losing money on his ferry. It became obvious that he would have to move or to quit. He and James H. Maxwell, Woodhull's successor, petitioned the Council to establish a ferry at the foot of Delancey Street; they also promised that, if the Council extended their lease for 21 years, they would agree to replace their horse ferry with steamboats by the end of three years. Cannon had moved out of the picture by this time. He had leased his ferry to John Gardner, who immediately asked the Council to refuse the petition of Willett and Maxwell. The matter hung fire from April to July. Despite Gardner's protests, the Council sided with Willett. On July 19 the Council had the "honor to present a lease to Marinus Willett and James Horner Maxwell for the ferry from Delancey Street Slip to Williamsburgh and also a deed of release from the Corporation to Col. Willett for the Lot of ground which was formerly conveyed by Col. Willett to the Corporation for the accommodation of the former ferry from Willett's Wharf."

The Martling Men

WHILE WILLETT WRANGLED WITH CANNON, De Witt Clinton had been doing nicely for himself. In addition to holding the Mayor's job from 1808 until 1810, he had also served as state senator. A persistent rumor pervaded New York City in 1811 that Clinton would again be appointed Mayor. An incensed group led by Mangle Minthorne, the father-in-law of Governor Tompkins, held a meeting at Martling's Tavern on February 4th. Despite considerable heckling by hired opposition, Minthorne and his cohorts succeeded in writing a memorial, protesting against the influence of the Clinton family in the Council of Appointments and requesting the legislature to make the Mayor's office elective. They suggested that if an appointment were to be made, either Nathan Sanford or Dr. Samuel L. Mitchell should receive it.

When Clinton again got the appointment, took the oath of office and left for Albany without appointing a deputy, the Minthorne contingent held a second meeting at Martling's at which they specified that Mayors of New York be elected annually at the same election with the charter officers. Candidates were to be citizens of New York state and inhabitants of the city for three years immediately preceding the election. The Mayor was to hold no other office and was to have his judicial authority removed.

The Clintonians accepted the challenge. They arrived early at a meeting in the Union Hall on William Street, took control of the gathering and tried to get all their resolutions passed before the opposition appeared. The latter had been warned. The Clintonians were driven out of the hall, though the sheriff and constables stood near the stage to defend their speakers. The Martling Men, as the followers of Minthorne were called, decided to fight to the death.

Up in Albany the president's chair in the senate room was shrouded in black. Members wore crepe on their left sleeves in respect for the memory of John Broome, who had departed this life. A successor had not been chosen. A special election was called for April 20 and on March 20 the news reached New York City that De Witt Clinton had received the nomination of the Republican party for the office of Lieutenant Governor to succeed Broome.

The Martling Men were beside themselves. What could Clinton want with an office which paid three thousand dollars a year when he was already getting nine or more for his job in New York? It did not take them long to put two and two together. Clinton was planning to hold both offices. He had done that sort of thing before. The Martling Men, as Republicans, would be expected to support him in his fight against Nicholas Fish, the Federalist candidate. They decided to bolt the party candidate and nominate a man of their own, so they met at Martling's on March 29 and announced that they could not support a "man whose continual accumulation of offices was subversive to the true principles of the Constitution." They sent a deputation to wait on Colonel Marinus Willett. Would he serve as their candidate for Lieutenant Governor? They returned with the news that Willett "considered himself bound to acquiesce in the wishes of his fellow-citizens upon the occasion."

The opposition newspapers seized upon Willett's nomination with glee. If the colonel had been infirm in 1807, what must he be now? The cries of Burrism rose. All of Willett's party shifting was aired by Charles Holt in *The Columbian*, the chief opposition newspaper. "Well we know," wrote Holt, "that Willett has been crawling beneath the legs of Federalist, Burrite, Fishite, Wortmanite, Davisite, Lewisite, alternately throughout the whole of his obscene public life. Let him be dubbed *Marinus the Twister.*" *The Public Advertiser,* the organ of the Martling Men, played up the colonel as the "Hero of Stanwix" and extolled him at great length for his deeds, often distorting history in its enthusiasm. This paper chose to forget the intervening years, but the opposition kept Willett's political record before the public. It could not stand up under the bombardment. Attempts to nominate the colonel in upstate communities failed miserably. Martin Van Buren, who was campaigning for Clinton, wrote that only one man in the county out of Clermont was supporting Willett and "whether he will get another vote for him is a subject much canvassed but doubtfull."

Willett was through as a political figure and the whole state knew it. Willett must have sensed it, too, for it is said that he told a friend from Otsego County that he had no illusions about winning the election but hoped to pull some votes away from Clinton. The end was sad indeed. In a state which gave between eighty and ninety thousand votes to Fish and Clinton, the "Hero of Stanwix" polled 3467. In the Mohawk Valley, where he had reached the peak of his military career, he received scant recognition. Herkimer County and Montgomery County each cast seven votes for the man who had preserved them from the Indians. These were "sticker" votes, for his name wasn't even on the ballots in those counties. Fish carried New York City but Clinton's popularity throughout the rest of the state won him the election.

The Martling Men were dead and so was Marinus Willett, as far as public office was concerned. He who had always followed a direct course on the battlefield had wound his way along the bypaths of his party, shifting his allegiance from one man to another until the electorate had no confidence in him as a leader. At the close he had gone down to one of the most humiliating defeats in the history of state elections. He must have known in his own heart that he deserved the blow which had been dealt him.

IV

TATTOO

1812 — 1830

Willett Lends Advice

THE WAR WAS STILL RAGING IN EUROPE. James Madison, whom Willett admired, was trying desperately to stave off an inevitable clash with Great Britain. The news of war reached New York on the morning of June 20, 1812, too late for publication in the newspapers. A public meeting was held in the Park four days later. Colonel Henry Rutgers, the tall bachelor who lived near Corlear's Hook, presided. Marinus Willett acted as secretary. The following resolutions were passed:

1. We have viewed with pleasure and approbation the necessary efforts of our government to preserve to our country her blessings of peace.
2. The crisis has arrived. We hold our government justified in its appeal to arms and yield our approbation.
3. It is the duty of good citizens to lay aside party animosity and party bickering and give the government their undivided support.
4. Placing our reliance on the Most High, and soliciting his benediction in our just cause, we pledge to our government, in support of our beloved country, our lives, our futures, and our sacred honor.

Though the war was unpopular in New York, the city nevertheless saw the need of defense. Militia companies were augmented and the harbor fortifications were improved. Willett, with experience in the field and as Mayor of the city at the time when the fortification of the Narrows had first been considered, volunteered his advice and services. General Van Rensselaer wrote in reply: "I shall remember your counsel with gratitude and pleasure as a precious legacy from a soldier of your great experience." There is no record of Willett having gained an appointment.

Though war on land brought little success, we enjoyed triumph after triumph at sea, and several heroes were welcomed with open arms by the city. Yet the attacks on Canada continued to fare badly.

Willett wanted to be of help. He could no longer lead armed troops, but he could send letters to the President, suggesting ways and means of conquering the enemy. Madison evidently paid scant attention to the unsolicited advice, for Willett sent him a petulent letter on June 15, 1813. After asking the President to look at an address he had sent the preceding winter, Willett added: "Had the measures then suggested been adopted and properly executed, the Naval force of the enemy would have been destroyed by the last of May. The sailors from our ships of war might by this time be on their return to their ships. And the troops be Concentrating their force on our Northern frontiers ready to penetrate into lower Canada. It is possibly not yet too late to ensure a successfull Campaign. But to effect this our Maritim force on the Lakes should be so increased as to ensure success. A deficiency in this respect can admit of no apology. Our Frigates had better be all laid up untill this most important object is obtained."

Alas, the President had no time for the ideas of a prattling old man. New York, however, still considered Willett to be a military leader, despite its lack of faith in his political life. In the summer of 1814, at a crucial point in the war, the colonel was asked to address a meeting in the Park. He stood on the balcony of the new City Hall, near the spot where he had defended the Liberty Pole forty years before. Now he was no Burrite or Lewisite or Martling Man. He was Colonel Marinus Willett, supporter of the Constitution in a time of crisis.

"Three score and fourteen years have brought with them some bodily infirmities. Had it been otherwise, and that my strength of body had remained as unimpaired as my love for my country, and the spirit that still animates me, you would not, my friends, have seen me here this day: I should have been amongst that glorious band, that, on the waters of Erie and Ontario, have achieved so much fame and lasting glory for their country!

"A life of seventy-four years has afforded me opportunities of seeing many great and surprising changes. Fifty-eight years are now passed since I was a witness of press-gangs traversing these streets, and dragging men from their houses on board of ships of war! What a contrast between that time and this! Let those now reflect upon it, who, instead of thanking that kind Providence which delivered us from such oppressive domination, employ their whole power to weaken and subvert a government made by ourselves, and for ourselves—the fruit of our blood and toil! What spirit is this, that, in the present crisis of our country, can lead to measures so disgraceful? Shall we abuse and villify those men we have placed at the head of our affairs, because they do not act just as we are pleased to say they should?

"No, my fellow citizens, for it is justly stated in the address of the Common Council, that we are not, in the present situation of our country, to inquire into the wisdom of measures which resulted in the declaration of this war. It is a fact, that we are at war; and that that war has been undertaken agreeably to the Constitution of our country. Every man bound to support the Constitution of the United States is, therefore, bound to support the war because it is a Constitutional act, and such is the law of the land. But, had I power to detail, and you patience to hear, what I have known and observed of the haughty, cruel, and gasconading nation that makes war against us, your feeling would oustrip my words, and anticipate the voice and commands of authority. The terms I use towards our enemy are not mine alone, nor proceeding from the personal warmth of my individual character. Such were the sentiments of men as great as this or any nation can boast of—Washington and Franklin. Dr. Franklin delivered his opinions in his correspondence with Lord Howe; and those of General Washington I have had from his own lips.

"Forty years ago I was at a meeting of citizens assembled on this green. The acclamation then was 'join or die.' The unanimity of that day procured the repeal of some obnoxious laws; but the design of enslaving us was not relinquished. Troops were stationed throughout the colonies to carry the nefarious intention into execution. Many were the broils between the citizen and the soldier, for the spirit of the citizens was roused, and they viewed with just indignation the mercenary troops that were to overthrow their liberties. They were stung by the ingratitude of the nation to which they had yielded loyal obedience, and assisted in its wars with ardour and alacrity. But had the enemy then conquered us as we did them, how different would have been our situation this day! Reflecting on this, it seems to me almost incredible that there should be Americans that could espouse the cause of such an enemy. Of what stuff are such hearts made? Is it possible that any such should be amongst the sons of those who fought your battles, my fellow-citizens, and won your freedom?

"It was, in the war of the revolution, a favourite toast—'May every Citizen be a Soldier, and every Soldier a Citizen.' Our citizens must now again become soldiers, and those soldiers be good citizens—not parading soldiers, fellow-citizens, but fighting soldiers—soldiers willing and ready to encounter the hardships and fatigues of war. I am not what I have been; but such as I am, wherever the enemy seek to deal most destruction, there you may look for me. And as to this mistaken idea that American militia are unequal to the contest with British regulars, I am a living witness to the contrary. With militia I have encountered them. I have met them when their numbers were double mine; and I have routed and pursued them. You, my fellow-citizens, if you will, can do the same. There is no terror in them for brave men, who dare look them in the face, and lock the bayonet with them. Let those who would dismay you by the terrors of war, rather reflect upon the part they have had in encouraging your enemy; and though war, like pestilence, may have been visited upon nations for their crimes, yet against this enemy we have committed no offence. We bore with cruelty, injustice and oppression of that insolent nation, till it became insupportable.

"Instead, therefore, of cavilling at the measures or operations of the war, let us rather unite to banish envy, hatred and discord, from amongst us; and resolve with all our might, to resist that implacable enemy, who will never respect us till we again compel him so to do.

"Permit me, then, my fellow-citizens, to conclude with a chorus we were used to sing in the camp in days of much more danger:

"Let Europe empty all her forces,
We'll meet them in array.
And shout—Huzza—Huzza—Huzza,
For Life and Liberty."

A fortnight later the city was thrown into panic by the British attack upon the national capital. *The Columbian Gazette* outdid itself with a hysterical editorial: "Your capitol is taken! 13,000 British troops may have marched for Baltimore, and before this hour it may have fallen. Six days ago the people at Washington were in perfect security. In six days the same enemy may be at the Hook, and if they assail your city with a powerful force by land and by water, what will be your fate? Arise from your slumbers! Let every citizen arise and enroll himself instantly and prepare to defend our city to the last extremity! This is no time to talk! We must act, and act with vigor, or we are lost!"

New York was not attacked. The war came to a victorious close by the end of the year.

Cedar Grove

MARINUS WILLETT RETIRED TO CEDAR GROVE to enjoy his remaining years with his wife and five children. Margaret Bancker, his third wife, reached her 40th birthday in 1814. Marinus, born in 1802, was preparing to enter Columbia College. The colonel had similar plans for William Marinus, 11, Edward Marinus, 9, and Elbert Marinus, 6. Margaret, born in 1810, was still a small child. Cedar Grove offered excellent play facilities for the youngsters. The house was ample and the gardens stretched toward a river which provided swimming and boating, not only for the colonel's children but for the boys and girls of Corlear's Hook. And there were ripe peaches and watermelons in the summer. A travelling circus would occasionally pitch its tents near Cedar Grove. The children must have been happy in such surroundings.

The colonel had gone back to the religion of his father. St. Stephen's Church was built on Christie Street near Broadway in 1805. Though it was nearly a mile from Cedar Grove, it was handier than Trinity, so the Willett family attended the new church regularly. William Marinus, the serious child, was to become an Episcopal rector. The colonel planned to send him to England after his graduation from Columbia. Marinus, the eldest son, showed a decided inclination toward the study of medicine. The others were too young to choose a profession, but the colonel wanted to give them all the opportunities he had lacked in his own youth. He felt that his political career would have been more successful had he been an educated man.

He was quite wealthy. He had held political offices which had rewarded him well financially, as he had been successful in adding those emoluments which accompanied his duties as Mayor and High Sheriff. His investments in land had turned out well. He had disposed of much of his large holdings in upstate New York at a profit. He had developed the Corlear's Hook area and had waited patiently for the city to reach him before parting with most of his land at figures far exceeding the purchase price. For example, four of six lots he had purchased in 1784 for less than $500 brought him $2300 in 1804. His annual income approached $5000, a sum which enabled him to entertain in lavish manner and to provide every comfort for his wife and children. Though his political career had not been an unqualified success, he had established himself financially as one of the substantial citizens of New York.

His children grew up in an excellent environment and their lives bore fruit which was already ripening when the colonel passed on. Marinus took his A. B. degree from Columbia in 1819 and his medical degree four years later. He established himself in New York, where he had an office first on West Broadway and later at 3 Harmon Street, where he died in 1840. William Marinus entered the ministry, but not in the manner prescribed by his father. After spending two years at Columbia the young man heard John Summerfield, the famous Wesleyan preacher. He was converted to Methodism, gave up plans to go to England to study, and became a circuit rider in Suffolk County. Marinus Willett was furious, for he was not accustomed to having his orders disobeyed. He disowned his son, who continued his career, first as a preacher and later as professor of Hebrew at Wesleyan University. Willett repented his severity. The father and son were reunited several years before the colonel's death. Edward Marinus became a lawyer in New York City, but Elbert died at the age of 26, before making any notable achievement which has been recorded. Margaret married James H. Ray. William and Edward both lived to be over 90, the former dying in 1895, the latter a year earlier. Margaret, the colonel's third wife and mother of the five children, passed away in 1867 at the age of 93.

Marinus Willett mellowed with age. Much of the fire had left him. He was even willing to forgive De Witt Clinton. In 1818 the colonel applied to the land office for 2000 acres of land as a reward for his services in the Mohawk Valley. Clinton, then Governor, notified him of the refusal of this grant and suggested that he apply to the legislature. In his reply, Willett did not berate either the Governor or the land office. He merely doubted the Commissioners' knowledge of the law. He commended Clinton for his recent speech to the legislature.

The two men were all too familiar with the problem of poverty in New York City. Willett agreed with Clinton that "the numerous institutions in the city had a tendency to increase the evil and to encourage idleness." Philadelphia was handling the problem better. Why couldn't New York adopt their method of dividing the city into districts with a commissioner to supervise each district?

Willett doubted if much could be done to regulate manufacture. Any move in that direction would "meet with insurmountable obstacles from the weakness and vanity of our citizens, Male and Female who are continually striving to excell each other in following foreign fashions."

Clinton's pet project, the Erie Canal, also came in for a word of advice. Willett had been interested in canals for many years. He wrote: "Great and important as the internal improvements by roads and canals would be to the state, the project of connecting the waters of Erie in the mode contemplated with the Hudson appears to me premature. It is like requiring a child who can scarcely lift fourteen pounds to carry fifty six. To effect this great work I think would requier trebly the present poppolation and resources of the State."

He inserted a reminder of the friendship which had existed between him and the Clinton family. He recalled that he had fought with the Governor's grandfather under Bradstreet many years before. He mentioned the intimacy between him and the Governor's uncle, George Clinton, when the latter was studying law in New York City before the Revolution, and the friendship which had been strengthened during the war and continued as long as George Clinton lived.

The colonel may have been thinking of Aaron Burr when he penned the closing paragraph: "Their might have been men in the United States of more briliant talents than George Washington and Governor Clinton But for sound minds good Judgment wholesome advise integrity and Candor, they are unrivaled. Your age, Sir, and your situation and tallents afford you opportunity of doing much towards raising a beautifull and lasting superstructure on that glorious foundation they were so greatly Instrumental in laying."

No record of a Clinton reply exists. Willett's claims to land were not recognized by the legislature. A few years later, before a group advocating Greek independence, Willett spoke in his familiar vein about the Sons of Liberty and their devotion to the cause of democracy. He may have had his tongue in his cheek when he offered the 2000 acres of land due him by the State of New York as his contribution to the Greek fund.

Though he had been rebuffed, the colonel did not relinquish his interest in politics. A Republican at heart, he had supported in turn the Sons of Liberty, the house of Clinton, and the more radical ideas of Aaron Burr. Though influenced by the earlier writings of Thomas Paine, he had refused to go all the way with that author's "Age of Reason." He had not wavered, however, in his devotion to the principles of Thomas Jefferson. He had supported the embargo despite opposition in New York by the Clintons and most of the citizens. He had come out to lend vocal support and had written advice to James Madison during the second war with Great Britain. He had welcomed James Monroe enthusiastically on his visit to New York in 1817.

The appearance of Andrew Jackson on the political scene brought a new note into Republican politics. Willett, the aged landowner, could not stomach this upstart from Tennessee. He played no part in the reception to Jackson given by the Sons of Tammany. He worked for the election of John Quincy Adams in 1824. As chairman of the New York delegation, he cast the vote that gave the state's support to the son of John Adams, the Federalist. And in 1828, the eighty-eight year old veteran of the Revolution presided at a meeting of that group of Republicans in the city which opposed Jackson's principles.

The fight against Jackson was to no avail. Willett, like many of the older citizens of the seaboard states, did not see the trend toward a new kind of democracy, a system far removed from the principles of Thomas Jefferson. Willett, who had been considered one of the most violent radicals in 1775, had lived long enough to find himself one of the arch-conservatives of 1828. He was too old to understand the evolution in politics through which his country was passing.

Lafayette

"HAIL, patriot, statesman, hero sage!
Hail freedom's friend! hail Gallia's son—
Whose laurels greener grow with age,
Pluck'd by the side of WASHINGTON!
Hail, champion in a holy cause,
When hostile bands our shore beset;
Whose valour bade th' oppressor pause—
HAIL, hoary warrior, LA FAYETTE!"

THE MORNING OF AUGUST 16, 1824 found Marinus Willett aboard the steamboat *Chancellor Livingston,* whose whistle was sounding departure from Castle Garden. General Clarkson had arrived, as had Colonels Varick, Platt and Trumbull, but where was Van Cortlandt? News of the arrival of Lafayette on Staten Island had been sent up the Hudson to the general's home. It was ten o'clock and the boat's captain could wait no longer.

A clatter of hoofs on the paving stones. A blur of horse and rider. A frantic shout from the pier. Philip Van Cortlandt had arrived with all the energy of his 80 years. He had ridden since early morning. Was he tired? Not a bit. He wasn't an old man like Marinus Willett.

The day was clear, the harbor calm. The *Chancellor Livingston* swung into the river, her decks lined with functionaries and veterans. Behind her paddled the *Robert Fulton,* carrying 200 tars from the frigate *Constitution.* Four gaily-decorated steamers trailed the sister ships. Bands played from the decks, which were crowded with passengers who had paid a dollar apiece for the privilege of welcoming the French nobleman. Small harbor craft bobbed and weaved between the larger ships.

Lafayette, who had spent the night at the home of Daniel Tompkins on Staten Island, met the *Chancellor Livingston* at the pier. He was dressed like a republican; nankeen pantaloons, buff vest and a plain blue coat set off his erect figure; in his hand he carried a new hat. He saw the veterans at the rail and waved them greeting. Colonel Platt, who had served in the Frenchmen's regiment during the war, rushed to the pier to embrace his friend. Platt did not monopolize Lafayette's attention. With a wave of his hand he indicated the other veterans and said, "Van Cortlandt, Willett, Varick and others are anxious and impatient to meet you."

Lafayette embraced them all affectionately, but it was Marinus Willett, the oldest soldier of the group, whom he embraced time and time again. And Willett, on one of the few occasions in his life, gave way to tears. Lafayette, ignoring everything else, pulled up a chair beside the aged colonel and engaged him in conversation which occupied most of the passage across the harbor, while the other veterans listened, nodding their approval as vivid stories rolled from the lips of the frontier colonel and the nation's guest.

Marinus Willett grew young again as he fought over in idea the battles of the Revolution. "Do you remember?" he asked, recalling the first time he had seen Lafayette. "It was at the battle of Monmouth. I was volunteer aide to General Scott that day. I saw you in the heat of battle. You were but a boy, but you were a serious and sedate lad."

Lafayette did remember. Hadn't it been Marinus Willett who had ridden over to Washington and his staff and pointed out to them their exposed position on the field? Much water had passed under the bridge since that hot day in 1778, but Lafayette remembered.

"Aye, aye," he answered, "I remember well."

"And on the Mohawk, I sent you fifty Indians and you wrote me that they set up such a frightful yell that they frightened the British horses and they ran one way and the Indians the other?"

Yes, it was all clear to the Frenchman. There had been the trip to the Mohawk Valley to hold council with the Indians. And Willett had helped de Tousard to procure an Indian boy for the Marquis to take back to France. Did Willett remember?

Could Willett ever forget those stirring days? He had lived far beyond his contemporaries. There wasn't much left for him; but the attention paid him by the honored guest filled him with the deepest happiness. The trip across the harbor was far too short.

New York entertained Lafayette for several days. There were theater parties, receptions in the City Hall, speeches and toasts. The Frenchman left for a tour of New England, but came back in time for the 67th anniversary of his birth, September 6th.

The Society of the Cincinnati, of which Lafayette was a member, entertained him at Washington Hall. Hundreds of veterans and sons of veterans came to do homage to the man who had left home and fortune to cast his lot with a cause which he had believed to be just. Of the old First New York regiment which had marched with Montgomery only four were present; Captain Willett, Captain Varick, Lieutenant Platt and Lieutenant Bleecker. McDougall, that fiery Son of Liberty, was but a cherished memory. Goose Van Schaick, who had led the expedition against the Onondagas, had been dead for 40 years. Young Peter Gansevoort, the love-sick defender of Fort Stanwix, had been buried in Albany in 1812. Yes, Marinus Willett had outlived his generation.

Many toasts were given, set toasts prepared by the committee. Lafayette arose and raised his glass amid a tense silence. "The sacred principles for which we have fought and bled," he cried, "Liberty, Equality, National Independence—may every nation of the earth in adopting them drink a bumper to the old Continental Army."

Thunderous cheers rang against the walls.

Several voluntary toasts were offered by younger men who had not fought in the Revolution but whose spirit had been aroused by the gallant Frenchman. Yorktown was toasted and Saratoga and Monmouth and the Brandywine. What about the heroes who fought on the frontiers, those men who had sacrificed their lives, their property and their ambitions in order to be of service to their country?

Marinus Willett was the oldest man in the gathering. They were calling on him for a toast. Before his eyes danced the figure of a gallant soldier who lay against the pillows smoking his pipe and joking with his visitor while his life blood ebbed slowly away.

The aged colonel rose. The glass trembled in his hand, but there was no weakness in his voice as he shouted, "The memory of General Herkimer and the militia who inhabited the country during our revolutionary war; their bravery and sufferings deserve to be remembered by this country."

He did not attend all the festivities in honor of Lafayette. He was too old and tired. There were fireworks at the Vauxhall Gardens, a visit to the Free Public School and a grand Masonic festival. At last it was over, and Lafayette was to leave for the South. Willett would see his friend no more.

Lafayette had not forgotten the old warrior. The morning before his departure he came to Cedar Grove and visited with Willett in the latter's garden. This thoughtfulness was something Willett cherished during the remaining years of his life.

Farewell

THE VETERAN spent more and more time in the beautiful garden behind the house he had planned for Mary Pearsee nearly a half century before. The trees they had planted now cast a grateful shade over his head as he limped along the garden path examining the melons he prized so much. The peach trees, too, were bearing quantities of the fruit he cherished. It was pleasant to sit in his chair and rest. Old friends came to share his reminiscences. Newspapers sent representatives to have him verify events of three-quarters of a century. Letters came, written by local historians, asking him to describe battles in which he had participated.

Appeals also arrived from comrades upon whom life had cast a frown. One of the soldiers who had been captured at Fort Stanwix while trying to get water from the spring had been reduced to "one pocket knife, two fowls and five gallons of vinegar." He was too old to work in the fields and must have a pension. Young William Finck of Capt. Bleecker's company, a boy who had been granted his release by Willett after the siege of Fort Stanwix so that he could go back to his harvesting, wrote a pathetic letter. He and his wife had little clothing. One of his children was subject to fits and unable to support himself. Due to a sore leg Finck was forced to walk with a crutch. He had no real estate and could not earn a living. He was 71 years old.

Willett's mind shifted back with the ease of the aged. He

saw Billy Finck standing before him, eighteen years old, smiling, handsome, his tousled yellow hair shining in the sun, his gray eyes pleading for a release. He had procured a substitute. Could he go back to his farming before the harvest was over? Now Billy was an old man, infirm and penniless. A tear rolled down Willett's cheek as he signed the pension request.

The old soldier spent much time writing his reminiscences. He penned them on long sheets of paper, in a hand that was still firm despite his age and infirmities. William Marinus promised to collect the papers after his father's death and publish the story of the colonel's military career. The book was to be dedicated to the Marquis de Lafayette.

Thoughts also entered Willett's mind that were not related to the battlefield. He pondered on his religious training, his waverings during middle life and his final return to the Episcopal Church. He recalled the teachings of Dr. Livingston, the preacher who had said to him fifty or more years before, "Contentment is to be found everywhere—or nowhere." Willett dwelt on that statement for a long time before grasping his pen and writing his philosophy of life:

"To be content and have a quiet mind are qualities worthy of our incessant pursuit and in proportion to the advancement will be the comfort obtained. Contentment and quiet are an harvest worth labouring for. They will pay as they go. To anticipate evils indicates weak intellect but the exercise of forethought by adopting measures to prevent futer evils is wise. In all events however contentment and a quiet mind will be found sources of comfort of as high a grade as we can hope to obtain as long as we remain on this world of sin & misery. By a regular deportment through divine aid we may reasonably hope at such a degree of patience as will result in such a measure of quiet & contentment as to prove the importance of these great qualities."

His reminiscences completed, Willett wrote his last document: "I Marinus Willett being upwards of Eighty six years of age, considering the uncertainty of this mortal life and knowing that my time here must be very short, do make this my last will and testament." To his beloved wife, Margaret, he bequeathed his cows, horses, carriages, plate, household furniture and garden utensils at Corlear's Hook, also $1500 in cash and one third of the interest and rents of his entire estate for her maintenance and support. She also was to have the privilege of occupying Cedar Grove during her lifetime. In addition she was left four lots fronting in Grand Street at the northwest corner of Cannon Street, one lot fronting on the west side of Cannon Street, five lots fronting on the east side of Willett Street and two lots fronting on the north side of Grand Street. To his eldest son, Marinus Willett, the colonel bequeathed the sword presented to him by Congress for his gallantry at Fort Stanwix. The residue of the estate was to be divided among his five children, the issue of his present wife. The share of Margaret, then under age, was to be under the guardianship of her mother, with the condition that when and if the girl married, the share was to be hers alone, without intervention on the part of her husband. The document was dated November 25, 1826.

The old warrior was downed by a stroke of paralysis in the spring of 1830. With resistance that was amazing in a man of ninety summers, he recovered and was able to sit in his garden. His only trouble was a persistent constipation. The doctor had left medicine for him, but he waved it aside. Of what use was it to prolong life now? He had seen all his comrades pass away. Even De Witt Clinton, his political rival, had been honored by a resolution from the Society of Cincinnati upon his death in 1828. Clinton had been born 30 years after Willett, who had fought with his grandfather and with his father, James Clinton.

Independence Day came, the 54th anniversary of the Declaration of Independence. Willett had heard the original declaration read in The Fields before George Washington.

He had prepared a parade ground on the shores of Otsego Lake so that the third anniversary could be celebrated properly by Clinton's brigade. He had marched with the Society on innumerable anniversaries. He had drunk toasts to Presidents from Washington to John Quincy Adams. He could not attend this year. He would prefer to sit in his garden.

A messenger, Horatio Gates Stevens, arrived, bringing a note from the Society which he read to Willett: "The Society congratulates you upon the return of our national anniversary, they feel grateful that an overruling Providence has permitted you to live to witness this 54th anniversary, but while they regret that your infirmities have not permitted you to join your brothers in the public celebration of the day, they are fully sensible that no one feels a deeper interest in the prosperity and happiness of the nation than yourself. The members of the Society assure you of their affectionate regard and profound respect."

Marinus Willett died on August 23, 1830, the 53d anniversary of the flight of St. Leger from before Fort Stanwix.

The frontier colonel lay in his coffin, clad in his street clothes, his black hat upon his head. He lay in his garden, surrounded by the flowers and vegetables he had prized so much, shaded by towering trees which had been planted by his own hands. He had requested this simplicity. A half century earlier he might have desired to have been buried in the gray and green regimentals of the Third New Yorkers. They had been part of his life, the most glorious part. But now, after so many years, he had tired of war. He had seen the nation through the most critical period of its history. A Republican at heart, he had lived to witness the transition from aristocracy to democracy. It often had been difficult for him. He might have done many things differently. But, despite conflicts and animosities, the nation had emerged at peace with the world. For this he had been grateful. He would be buried, not as a military conqueror, but as a man of peace.

So he lay there, in his garden, while the people passed by in tribute to the citizen they loved and respected. Ten thousand of them came; they formed a procession which stretched far into the streets.

The service was simple, as Marinus Willett had wished it to be. Dr. De Witt, a friend of long standing, offered a short prayer, alluding to the exploits of the man who had been a fellow officer of his father. The procession was led by a troop of militia with a band. The Society of the Cincinnati marched, as did members of the Court of Magistrates. The long journey to Trinity Church was made through streets lined with citizens. Night had fallen when the mourners reached Broadway. The coffin was taken from the hearse some distance from the church and surrounded by brother officers, who bore it through a lane of soldiers into the church. After a brief prayer by Mr. Anthony, the body was carried to the graveyard. Tapers were lighted to guide the mourners. Muffled drums sent dull reverberations through the graveyard. In the distance the minute-guns from the Battery boomed ninety times. A volley of musketry. Marinus Willett had gone to his reward.

"*The Hero of Fort Stanwix is no more!* He has fought the good fight—he has finished his course, and henceforth we hope there is a crown of glory in store for him."

Bibliography

Willett Manuscript Material

Diary of the Creek Mission. Tomlinson Collection. New York Public Library.
Letters and Papers. General Manuscript Collection. New-York Historical Society.
Letters and Papers. Emmett Collection. New York Public Library.
Letters to General Horatio Gates. Gates Collection. New-York Historical Society.
Letters to John Lamb. Lamb Collection. New-York Historical Society.
Letters to General Philip Schuyler. Schuyler Papers. New York Public Library.
Orderly Book, February 18, 1777 to May 20, 1778. Tomlinson Collection.
Papers, 1778 to 1783. Tomlinson Collection.
Regimental Orders, 1781. Tomlinson Collection.
Reminiscences. Tomlinson Collection. (Missing sheets are to be found in the Morgan Collection, New York Public Library.)

Newspapers Consulted

New York American Citizen, 1804-1807. (James Cheetham)
New York American, 1830.
New York Argus, or Greenleaf's New Daily Advertiser, 1795.
New York Commercial Advertiser, 1830.
New York Evening Post, 1807. (William Coleman)
New York Morning Chronicle, 1807. (Peter Irving)
New York Packet and the American Advertiser, 1784, 1785.
New York Public Advertiser, 1807.
New York Journal or the Daily Advertiser, 1774-1776. (John Holt)
New York Journal and Patriotic Register, 1790-1791. (John Holt)
New York Journal or the Weekly Register, 1781-1790. (John Holt)
New York Republican Watch Tower, 1807. (Thomas Farmer)

Most Important Secondary Sources

Barnes, Elinor. *The First Federal City. New York in 1789*. Proceedings of the New York State Historical Association. Vol. XXXVIII. New York History. Vol. XXI. 1940. pp. 162-179.

Clinton, George. *Public Papers of George Clinton, First Governor of New York*. State of New York. 10 vols. 1899-1914.

Cook, Frederick. *Journals of the Military Expedition of Major-General John Sullivan against the Six Nations of Indians in 1779*. Auburn, N. Y. Knapp & Co. 1887.

Colbrath, William. *Journal of the most Material Occurrences Preceeding the Siege of Fort Schuyler (formerly Fort Stanwix) with an Account of that Siege, &c*. Photostat in New York Public Library, from manuscript owned in 1926 by Dr. A. W. S. Rosenbach, New York City.

Greene, Nelson. *A History of the Mohawk Valley, 1614-1925*. Chicago. The S. J. Clarke Publishing Company. Vols. I and II.

Headley, J. T. *The Great Riots of New York*. New York. E. B. Treat. 805 Broadway. 1873.

Jones, Thomas. *A History of New York during the Revolutionary War*. New York. Printed for The New-York Historical Society. 2 vols. 1879.

Leake, Isaac Q. *Memoir of the Life and Times of General John Lamb*. Albany. Joel Munsell. 1850.

Lefferts, Lieut. Charles M. *Uniforms of American, British, French and German Armies in the War of American Revolution*. New York. New-York Historical Society. 1926.

O'Callaghan, E. B. *The Documentary History of the State of New York*. Albany, N. Y. Weed, Parsons & Co. 4 vols. 1849.

Pomerantz, Sidney I. *New York, An American City, 1783-1803*. New York. Columbia University Press. 1938.

Scott, John Albert. *Fort Stanwix and Oriskany*. Rome, N. Y. Rome Sentinel Company. 1927.

Simms, Jeptha. *The Frontiersmen of New York*. Albany, N. Y. Geor. C. Riggs. 2 vols. 1882.

Willett, William M. *A Narrative of the Military Actions of Colonel Marinus Willett, taken chiefly from his own manuscript*. New York. G. & C. & H. Carvill. 1831.

Index